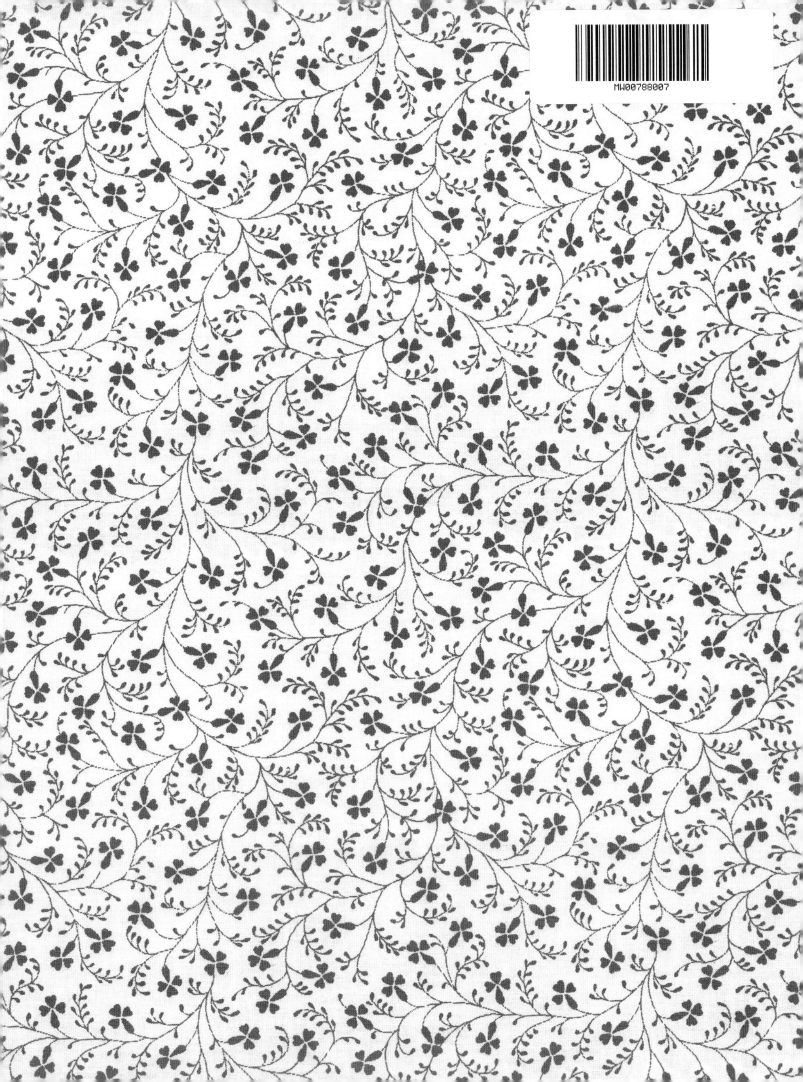

LAURA ASHLEY

MARTIN WOOD

LAURA ASHLEY

MARTIN WOOD

F

FRANCES LINCOLN LIMITED
PUBLISHERS

Frances Lincoln Limited, 4 Torriano Mews, Torriano Avenue,
London NW5 2RZ   www.franceslincoln.com

Laura Ashley

First Frances Lincoln edition 2009

ISBN 978-0-7112-2897-9

Printed and bound in China

1 2 3 4 5 6 7 8 9

ENDPAPERS: 'Campion' pattern R143. A long-produced and
much-loved pattern.

FRONTISPIECE: Oriana Baddeley, taken in Paultons Square, London, 1973.

THIS PAGE: A picnic. From left, Sara, Nick, Robina, Laurel and 'GC'.

For one who had a verdant heart

CONTENTS

Cae-Harris, Dowlais

Caeharris Pond, Dowlais, as
Laura would have known it.
Ifor Works is in the distance,
with Muriel Terrace to the
right. Station Terrace, where
Laura was born, is further
to the right just out of the
picture.

FROM THE LAND OF MYTH AND SONG

There is perhaps one name amongst the many on the high street that stands out, unique and much loved: that of Laura Ashley. The story of Laura Ashley is a fascinating one. It is not just a story about the creation of a multi-million-pound business with hundreds of shops all over the world, nor is it just the portrait of a remarkable lady who died more than twenty years ago and whose name is now famous for fashion and home furnishings. It is really the story of a quite extraordinary partnership. Laura and Bernard Ashley were a remarkable couple. Together they opened a chain of shops, and numerous factories to supply them – many in rural Wales – bringing jobs, prosperity and hope to many communities. But just who was Laura Ashley and how is it that her name has become so familiar to people today as a high street brand?

To discover Laura Ashley we must make a journey to Wales, the land of myth, of legend, and of song, with its deep valleys and soaring mountains. Laura was born Laura Mountney on 7 September 1925 at her grandmother's house, 31 Station Terrace, Dowlais, Merthyr Tydfil, in South Wales. Laura recalled, 'I was born in Dowlais – what they call Dowlais Top. It's a terrace right at the very top of the hill on the south side of the Brecon Beacons, very exposed and bitterly cold.'[1] Throughout her life Wales and her Welsh roots proved to be of profound importance to Laura. Perhaps more than anything else it was to define her and to make her who she was, for paradoxically it enabled her to seem the embodiment of an English lady. She explained: 'Being Welsh, I can look at England objectively. I think the architecture, furniture and art of England are very beautiful – and I can appreciate it all the more from the vantage of being tucked away in the Welsh mountains.'[2] Perhaps she had a point; as Kipling wrote, 'What should they know of England, who only England know?'

Laura wasn't wholly Welsh: her father, Lewis Stanley 'Frank' Mountney (1896–1966), was partly English, from a Staffordshire family where, together with South Derbyshire, Mountneys had been settled for generations. Laura's great grandfather, John Mountney, was a butcher at Doveridge near Sudbury in Staffordshire. His son, Francis

Charles Mountney (Laura's grandfather), became a trooper in the 2nd Life Guards stationed at Regents Park Barracks. The family history becomes rather complicated, for Francis Mountney married Mary, Laura's maternal grandmother's half sister, so her parents were distant relations.[3]

Laura's father was brought up in London and became a civil servant in the War Office, living most of his life in suburbia in Wallington, Surrey. But it was to be Wales and the Welsh ancestry of her mother's family, which was to have a lasting influence on Laura. Her mother, Margaret Elizabeth Davies (1905–1992), was born at 7a Charlotte Street, Dowlais. Laura's grandfather, Enoch John Davies, was a policeman in Merthyr Tydfil, although in later life he became a warehouseman. He was of farming stock; the Davies family had farmed at Southlays, Rudbaxton, not far from Haverfordwest in Pembrokeshire, for generations. Laura's

grandmother, Margaret Benyon, came from an old Welsh family and her father, Lewis Benyon, was described on her marriage certificate as an iron founder. He certainly could neither read nor write for on the certificate he made his mark with an 'x'.

There is a strong economic divide between North and South Wales. In the eighteenth and nineteenth centuries the south became largely industrial. Coal deposits fuelled iron working, and these activities shaped the landscape and also the character of the people. It also fuelled immigration, so the south had fewer Welsh-speaking inhabitants than were to be found in the north or mid-Wales, where there was precious little industry aside from slate quarries. Some remnants of this activity survive in the north but then, as now, both North and mid-Wales relied on farming and on tourism. It was grazing country, not arable land, with sheep in the majority, while the magnificent castles, built by Edward I along the north

ABOVE: Station Terrace, Dowlais Top, where Laura was born.

OPPOSITE: Laura (centre) with her parents and (from left) Trevor, Francis and Mary.

Wales coast, together with the dramatic landscape, made it both a traveller's and painter's dream.

Laura's parents, who were married in 1924, lived in Camden Road in Holloway, but when Laura was four her parents decided to buy a new house in Beddington Park, Wallington, near Croydon in Surrey. Following the First World War there was a boom in house building, mostly aimed at providing better houses for the lower middle class – the fulfilment of the promise of 'a land fit for heroes'. Property was relatively cheap and some of those suburban semi-detached homes were occasionally referred to as postman's houses, simply because it cost a postman a year's wages to buy one. Laura's father had been persuaded to buy a house in the area by his brother, Ivor, who lived nearby, as did their sister Elsie, who was to play a major role in Laura's life. Laura was the eldest of four children – Laura, Mary, Francis and Trevor. The youngest, Trevor, was a rather sickly child and this necessitated visits to hospital in London. Laura would often be left in the care of her Aunt Elsie, who was childless. Laura had her own room at her aunt's, which helped to relieve some of the pressure on her mother. Her aunt spoilt her, buying her the odd dress from Liberty and other such treats. It was a rather genteel world or, perhaps more correctly, one of middle class propriety.

Holidays were usually spent in Wales, with Laura and her sister Mary being put on a train at Paddington, in the charge of the guard. She would eat her scrambled egg and cress sandwiches as the train sped along the English countryside, passing through the Severn tunnel – 'holding my breath because I was afraid of the dark then' – before the train drew into Newport in South Wales.[4] There her grandmother would be standing waiting – 'she was thin and as neat as a governess in her black tailored suit and white blouse, a straw hat and healthy country face'. Together they would wait for the Brecon train in the refreshment rooms, all 'white tiles, marble tops and gleaming mahogany, and I was always given just a glass of milk'.[5]

Station Terrace was a tiny house, basically a two up, two down. The atmosphere must have been very different from that at her Aunt Elsie's: a sort of working class respectability, although underpinned by Welsh non-conformity. The rosy glow of nostalgia often casts a deceptive light, particularly on childhood memories, when we are all apt to forget days when it rained and the sun didn't shine. In later years Laura was to recall that her grandparents 'were very strict, but very happy'. Laura's abiding memory of the house was that it was 'very scrubbed and polished', and each 'morning the step had to be whitened and the brasses polished'.[6] Although Enoch and Margaret Davies had been married in St David's Church under the Established (Anglican) Church, Margaret certainly worshipped at the nearby Hebron Chapel, which was Baptist. Sunday's were devoted to religion and going to chapel. 'You dressed quite differently on a Sunday' and after breakfast, done up in their Sunday best, they all made their way down the hill to the chapel, as they did 'three times a day, and Sunday school in the afternoon was for everybody, not just children, so you could have elderly people in the Sunday School classes.' Laura was to recall that the services, together with the very long sermons, were 'all in Welsh which I couldn't understand'.[7] Throughout her life religion, though perhaps not in a formal organised sort of way, was of profound importance to Laura and it underpinned much of what she thought and did. She once remarked, a 'great thing I learnt from my childhood was that the Devil is as real as God, and I think that is a quite important thing to remember'.[8]

Laura's great-aunt, Jessica (one of her grandmother's sisters), had asthma, and had been advised to take the air. So 'everyday at 11 o'clock all my great-aunts would set off to the Twyniau, which was a great rocky outcrop up in the mountains'.[9] John Lloyd, one of the husbands, would join them. 'He would only discuss religion – he would not talk about anything else – so the whole walk from 11 a.m. to 3 p.m. was religion. It was rather like being in the wilderness

up there.'[10] At least they had the presence of mind to take some sandwiches, but the weather was usually so inclement that the walk was often conducted in the pouring rain. Laura's abiding memory was 'crouching behind granite boulders out of the howling wind to try and eat our sodden sandwiches'.[11]

On 3 September 1939, just after 11 o'clock in the morning, the Prime Minister, Neville Chamberlain, announced on the BBC Home Service that the government's demand for Germany to withdraw its forces from Poland had met with no response: 'I have to tell you now', his sombre voice intoned, 'that no such undertaking has been received and consequently this country is at war with Germany.' Wallington lay rather too close to Croydon aerodrome, which was bound to be a target for German bombing, so 'my Mother hustled us all back to Wales – the four of us – and we had to spend the first night in Cardiff because there was a terrific rush to Wales that particular night: the trains were packed. We had to spend the first night in a cupboard because she was so frightened the bombs were going to fall that night.'[12] The tiny house at Dowlais was bursting at the seams with no less than ten people camped out there. Grandma Wales, as they called her, had rented a wireless so everyone was able to gather round and listen to Alvar Liddell reporting news of the war on the BBC Home Service, and the majority of it in those early days of the war was bleak to say the least.

Laura was thirteen when war broke out and her formal education effectively ended, because they found that 'Dowlais was absolutely flooded with the Folkestone Grammar School and they filled all the schools'. Of course everyone had to make a contribution to the war effort and it was decided that Laura 'had better take a secretarial course, so I had to go across the mountain to Aberdare' to a secretarial college. The mass blanket bombing which everyone had expected at the beginning of the war did not materialize (at least not in those early months), and so many people, including Laura's parents, brought their children back to London, and as it turned out, to danger.

Her father, though not an old man, was in frail health, so after a year in Wales Laura returned to look after him. The secretarial training continued at the Pitman College in Croydon, but in 1941 she joined the Girls Training Corps (GTC) and then at seventeen got a job as a shorthand typist at the Ministry of Health. Her uncle had pulled a few strings to secure her the position, but in 1943 she joined the Woman's Royal Naval Service (WRNS, popularly and now officially known as the Wrens). She began her basic training at Mill Hill training depot in March 1944, and subsequently trained to use a teleprinter, learning the art of sending signals and messages in code. Thus began Laura's lifelong love of the telex, a now obsolete piece of office machinery. After passing out, Laura was sent to Southsea, and then to HMS *Dryad*, Allied Naval Combined Expeditionary Force (ANCXF) where, in utmost secrecy, the Normandy landings were being planned. Under the command of Admiral Ramsay, General Eisenhower and General (later Field Marshal) Montgomery were often seen at the house, as was Winston Churchill, and on at least one occasion even the King himself.[13]

After the Normandy landings on 4 June 1944 Laura was in the first party of Wrens personnel to cross to France. She was nineteen and this was her first trip abroad. Landing at Arromanches, the British Mulberry harbour, they were sent to Granville. Soon after, they were sent to work in Paris, billeted in a chateau that had been used by German officers, necessitating a large bonfire of portraits of Hitler and other assorted Nazi paraphernalia. Soon they moved again, this time to Brussels where they were based at Allied headquarters in the Hotel Metropole, not quite as chic as Paris, but closer to the front line. When the Germans launched their ill-fated counter-attack through the Ardennes, it looked as though the Wrens might have to be withdrawn, but in the event Hitler and his panzers were roundly defeated and the war drew towards its inevitable close. Laura did not venture into Germany – parental consent was required for her deployment as she was underage, and this was not forthcoming – so she

returned to Britain and was demobilized in August of 1946. She found a job in the city as an averages assessor, for Laura was something of a mathematician.[14]

The war changed and touched everyone's lives, and it is perhaps understandable that after so much suffering people wanted to get on with living their lives. Laura was no exception. In 1943, at the age of eighteen she had joined a local youth club in Wallington where she met Bernard Ashley at a Rugby Club dance. Tall, good looking and a year younger than Laura, he was in many ways everything Laura was not. He was outgoing and gregarious or, as Laura remarked, 'he was a bit wild'. She was quiet and more reserved. She recalled, 'We met at a Rugby Club dance and he had come with a rugby ball because he thought it might be rather boring and it might liven up the proceedings if he actually started a game on the dance floor, which he promptly did.' Laura wisely withdrew and 'crouched behind a piano because I'm of a rather nervous disposition. I don't know how he ever noticed me.'[15] Wild he might have been, but the attraction must have been instant for in later life Laura remarked, 'The minute I set eyes on him I knew that this was the man I wanted to spend the rest of my life with.'[16] Unbeknown to Laura, Bernard had already noticed her standing on Wallington Station. She stood out because she 'didn't look like other girls, with semi court shoes and socks to her knees'.[17] Not wishing to seem too keen she made Bernard woo her. In later years Bernard was to recall that he 'had met a young Wren, a telex operator, with whom he fell in love'. Laura gave Bernard the impression that she was very keen on a dashing young Major. Bernard went off to India with his regiment and although they remained in contact 'Laura hadn't written very much'.[18] He returned to England in 1946 and after being demobilized in 1947 he went straight to Laura and asked her to marry him. She said yes. Years later Bernard discovered that the Major was just a myth. Laura had known even then that rivalry would make Bernard keener.[19]

In many ways their family backgrounds were not dissimilar. Bernard had been born above his parents' grocery shop in 99 Beechdale Road, Brixton on 11 August 1926.[20] Not long after he was born his parents acquired another grocers in Wallington, where they moved, although they retained the Brixton shop as well, which Bernard's father ran. Bernard's grandfather had also been in the grocery business and had owned two shops: one in North London and one in Catford, both selling dry goods. The shop next-door but one, complementing what the Ashleys sold by stocking dairy produce and game, was owned by Sainsburys, who would come and use the Ashley's telephone.

At the outbreak of war there was a slump in the value of property, particularly houses around strategic targets such as Croydon aerodrome, and so Bernard's parents were able to buy a detached house in the Newlands, Wallington. Hilda Ashley, Bernard's Mother, was an ambitious lady and a rather dominating character. Her father, Walter Woodward, owned a small engineering business, which was later run by Bernard's grandmother.[21] Originally from Norfolk, the Woodwards had manufactured farm machinery (primarily threshing machines although even today a few traction engines survive bearing the 'Woodward and Copeline' name), but had gone bankrupt in the nineteenth century. Starting over, they developed and patented an oil heater, which might sound rather unglamorous but was an essential piece of machinery when the Royal Navy converted the fleet from coal to oil.[22] It restored the family fortune. This was obviously the source of Bernard's fascination with machinery which he remarked, 'is in my DNA as I've always loved machinery'. He was fascinated by how machines worked and their capabilities, but also in building his own machines which he often did from Dexion, a sort of gigantic Meccano set. Bernard's grandmother, Mary Woodward, was extremely fond of Bernard and wanted to give him the family engineering business, based in Sutton and by then fairly small as most of the patents had expired.[23] In the end the business passed into other hands, but at least Bernard was taught how to turn on a lathe, a basic engineering skill that was to stand him in good stead in the future.

TOP: Mary and Walter Woodward, Bernard's grandparents.

BOTTOM: Bernard with his brother Geoffrey and their parents. Probably taken in late 1946.

Bernard was sent to a public school, Whitgift Middle (now known as Trinity School of John Whitgift), where, to his great pride, he succeeded in never passing a single exam, although he never gained the distinction of being bottom of the class. That honour consistently fell to another boy called Knowles. Thwarted in this worthy ambition Bernard nevertheless 'left school with a completely clear mind', proving Lady Bracknell's memorable observation that 'in England at any rate, education produces no effect whatsoever'.[24] Bernard was a practical rather than an academic sort of man, happier on the factory floor, and more at home amongst engineers and farmers than dealing with accountants and bankers.

Having failed to get into the RAF (he had wanted to be a pilot), in 1943 Bernard applied for a commission and was accepted into the Royal Fusiliers, being called up in August 1944. After training he became an officer in the 2nd battalion of the First Gurkha Rifles. Sent to India, he spent some time at Dharamsala, then a small Hill Station, but now better known as the residence of the Dalai Lama. After the end of the war he transferred to the Indian Army Service Corps (attached to Force 401 [Iran 1946/7]), considered in service terms to be the lowest of the low, but organising the movement of trucks was to be invaluable experience. Bernard recalled, 'India was my education', and it awakened an interest in philosophy and religion, fuelling a romantic dream to become a writer.[25]

Bernard returned to England in late 1946 and was eventually demobilized in November 1947. He got a job as a clerk with Goodlass Wall Ltd. (a paint company), but counting tins of paint all day was of limited appeal. He moved on to an import-export agent, which again did not really suit, and then was unemployed for a time. Eventually, in November 1948, he got a job as a personal assistant to a director of the Gallic Investment Co., a small, family-run investment company in the city where he stayed for four years.[26] In 1951 he became the company secretary, and in many ways this provided an excellent grounding as he learned a great deal about finance, all of which would come in handy in the future. Bernard was

Bernard riding in India in 1946.

OPPOSITE: Laura and Bernard
on their wedding day in 1949.

RIGHT: Laura and Bernard
at Club Méditerranée at
Piambino, Italy in 1952.

really a frustrated entrepreneur: at school this was already apparent with the two businesses he ran, one swapping Meccano and another selling textbooks, then an expensive and valuable commodity.[27]

His future was to be with Laura, and she and Bernard were married on 22 February 1949 at Beddington Park Church. The organist failed to turn up and the church was freezing cold. After the ceremony there was a small reception at the Grange Hotel and the newlyweds enjoyed a very short honeymoon in Alfriston. They began their married life in rented rooms in Cheam, but soon migrated to Chelsea, house-sitting for an elderly lady in Drayton Gardens while she visited her son in Australia. Upon her return they moved to an unfurnished flat in Pimlico. In March 1949 Laura took a new job as a secretary in the handicrafts department of the National Federation of Women's Institutes in Eccleston Square in nearby Victoria. She stayed with the WI until September 1952 when she left to become secretary to the First Secretary at the High Commission for Pakistan.[28] Bernard still nursed an ambition to be a writer – working in the city by day and writing by night – but the rejection letters continued to mount and he never actually published a word. They even changed flats, moving from the ground to the quieter attic floor in the same building, reached by climbing no less than ninety-nine steps. But when you are young, what are such trials?

THE
ROUNDABOUT
ONE PENNY

MADE IN ENGLAND

Laura Ashley HANDPRINT ON IRISH LINEN

18

KITCHEN TABLE CHIC

Various versions of how Laura Ashley the company began have entered into folklore. The truth is that it all began with patchwork, at a kitchen table in Pimlico. In the early 1950s Bernard and Laura had rented a flat at 56 St George's Square for £2 5*s*.[1] At first they lived on the ground floor, but with Bernard nursing an ambition to be a writer, and their neighbours in the basement being rather noisy, they moved to the attic on the fifth floor. In those days Pimlico was not the well-heeled area we see today. Rather, it was, as Bernard remarked, 'full of streets that are almost slums, others are just sordid and now and then there is a square and some green and some trees …. The pavements are fairly well covered by prostitutes, who look as if they have been relegated there from the West End …. There are a number of artists living near the Thames and on the whole it is a jolly place.'[2]

Working in the city by day and trying to write at night was pretty exhausting, so Bernard said to Laura, 'Can't you start a business and make money so I can write?'[3] They had various ideas, one was to sell Harris tweed in America, but it was to be a childhood memory that provided the inspiration. Laura's great grandmother, who had lived for a short time in America, had a quilting frame in her parlour and 'she used to make patchwork quilts for all and sundry, as well as having eight children. It was rather like Mrs Gaskell's *Cranford* actually.'[4] Naturally Laura was taught how to do patchwork, as well as all manner of needlework, and she had watched her grandmother and aunts making patchwork quilts as well as rag rugs. Working at the Women's Institute as a secretary in the handicrafts department Laura saw the scope, variety and the exceptional quality of many of the items produced. In March 1952 the WI organised an exhibition of handicrafts at the Victoria and Albert Museum, which included hand-printed and hand-woven fabrics, along with embroidery and patchwork items. Seeing what other women were doing at home Laura was determined to have a go herself. Looking around she found very few fabrics that she felt would be suitable. Patchwork, by its very nature, really needs small prints, tiny stripes and small weave textures, but they proved harder to find than might be imagined. In the early 1950s there was not the wide choice of

Victorian bathers tea towel, an early design, produced before the Ashleys moved to Wales, hence 'Made in England'.

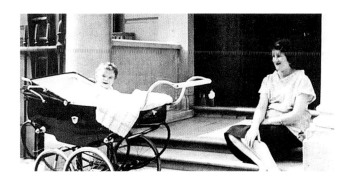

fabric we enjoy today. Most fabric had been rationed during the war, and for many years thereafter, with only simple twills off ration. Laura found it difficult to find what she needed, and so she began to research fabric printing, borrowing a book on the subject from the local library. In the spring of 1953 Laura was pregnant with their first child and was advised to rest as much as possible. Sewing was an obvious way to pass the time.

There are a variety of ways in which fabrics may be printed with a pattern. At its most basic one can cut a shape out of a potato and use that, or a piece of linoleum to be a tad more sophisticated. Most of us have done such things in art classes at school. This is basically a crude form of block printing. Today probably the most expensive method of producing a print is to use hand blocking. This method uses a series of blocks, which are pieces of wood with a pattern carved out in flat relief. It is quite usual for the intricate details (prone to wear out quickly or break off) to be worked in metal, such as brass or copper, a process known as 'coppering'. Sometimes, if the pattern is small and intricate the whole block might be 'coppered'. Each colour to be used requires a separate block that places the colour within the overall pattern. Such printing – the method also used to produce hand-blocked wallpapers – requires considerable skill by the printer. The fabric is stretched out along a table and each block has locator hooks at the side. These hooks match up to small holes in the selvedge of the fabric so each block can be positioned exactly. A similar amount of dye needs to be applied for each press, and a similar amount of pressure applied to the block. Therein lies the skill. Many complex floral prints (often mistakenly called chintzes) might have as many as ten or more blocks and it is usual for each colour to be printed in turn on the piece and the fabric allowed to dry between each blocking.[5] 'Hollyhocks', a famous old floral pattern still produced by Lee Jofa, requires no less than thirty-two blocks to produce. The process is laborious and very expensive, yet the end result is wonderfully rich in texture.

TOP: Laura with Jane outside 56 St George's Square.

ABOVE AND OPPOSITE: Printing blocks. These were probably wallpaper blocks, but the style of pattern is similar to what caught Laura's eye.

Another method is screen-printing and this is how the Ashleys began. In a way, it is similar to block printing. A screen is made, often of silk or nylon stretched over a metal frame (the Ashleys initially used wooden frames which have a tendency to warp), with the pattern blocked out using enamel. The colour is drawn across the screen by a squeeze thus transferring the pattern to the fabric. Again a separate screen is needed for each colour, but the whole process is not as slow as hand blocking. This is flat bed screen-printing. A far faster method is rotary screen-printing where the screens are mounted on cylinders and the colour is forced through the screen from the inside of the cylinder. You need as many rotary screens as colours, but the repeat size of the design is usually smaller than that which can be achieved with flatbed screens and is determined by the circumference of the roller.[6]

Copperplate printing is another method, similar in a way to hand blocking, devised in the eighteenth century and used in the printing of many *toile de Jouy* patterns. The design is etched onto large copperplates and is similar to the method used to print books. Gradually, it has been replaced by roller printing as this is more economic for large-scale production. The design is etched onto copper rollers and the fabric is passed around a large central roller with each colour roller arranged around the central roller. The colours are printed in sequence as the fabric is drawn around. One slight disadvantage of this method is that the fabric has no opportunity to dry between each colour application.

Today technology is gradually revolutionizing the business with digital fabric printing, and Bernard Ashley, with his company Elanbach Ltd., had been at the forefront of the industry. This process uses an inkjet printer (similar to an office or domestic paper printer only on a gigantic scale) with the design controlled from a computer CAD system. There is huge potential to re-colour and to re-scale a design simply and cheaply. The quality is not quite as crisp as a roller print and in many ways it more closely resembles the hand-blocked product. However, its great advantage is that it is economically viable for shorter bespoke runs, whereas the economics of producing screens for screen-printing means it is only viable for longer runs and used to require the purchase of two pieces – a full piece being some 60 yards in length.

On holiday in Italy in June 1953 the Ashleys had seen young women wearing neck scarves. Audrey Hepburn had noticed the trend, which had inspired her to wear them in the film *Roman Holiday*, premiered in New York in August 1953 (it had been filmed between June and September the previous year). These scarves were quite small – about 20 inches square – and so the Ashleys bought a few to bring home. They proved to be an ideal product, so they unashamedly copied them. Bernard photographed them and made a silk screen, all of which was done for the princely sum of £10. The kitchen table was pressed into service as a printing table, fitted out with a felt top over which was stretched a plastic cover. The dimensions of the table naturally limited the size of the printable area, so each piece of fabric was a single design. This arrangement was ideal not just for scarves, but also for tablemats, napkins and other small everyday household objects. Laura was drawn even then to small stripe and flower motifs, but these were far too intricate for the silk screens, so they adopted bold geometric patterns in striking colours. Some were inspired by abstract art, and one customer had enamel earrings made to similar designs, selling scarf and earrings as a set.[7]

The original scarves had a pattern of stars with a hole punched through the centre of each star. The Ashleys were using pigment dyes which had to be fixed by heat, so the gas oven was requisitioned for the purpose. Bernard made a rack from thick wire, but a sharp eye was required, as quite often some scarves at the back near to the burner could be scorched or singed. If not too badly charred they would be sold as 'seconds'. Bernard approached John Lewis, the Oxford Street department store, and although the buyer was rather hesitant he nevertheless came away with an order

OPPOSITE TOP: Automatic silk screen printing at the Laura Ashley factory in Carno, Wales.

OPPOSITE MIDDLE: A semi-automatic printer at Carno. This stripe design in shades of brown is one of Bernard's.

OPPOSITE BOTTOM: The printing heads of a modern digital printing machine.

ABOVE: Audrey Hepburn in the 1953 film *Roman Holiday* wearing a neck scarf similar to those copied by the Ashleys.

OVERLEAF: Tablemats, an early product. Cars were a popular subject, as were soldiers (see page 152) and bicycles.

1920 Riley 11

1920   G.N.   Twin

for a gross (twelve dozen). Two hours later the telephone rang: the scarves had sold out, at 3s. each, and a repeat order was placed. As many as a hundred scarves were being printed every evening, although there are no examples in the archives and none are known to have survived. Soon 'Ashley' products could be purchased at John Lewis, Woollands (a long defunct department store in Knightsbridge) and at Heal's on Tottenham Court Road.[8] Aside from raw materials – fabric was bought from a mill in Lancashire for £10 a roll (probably of 60 yards) – the greatest outlay was the gas to heat the oven. In the first year their turnover amounted to a staggering £2,000.[9] Initially Bernard delivered all the orders on his motorbike on the way to work, but later he used their one extravagance, a battered old van bought for £30.

On the strength of this success Bernard decided to leave his job in the city and devote all his time, and considerable energy, to the embryonic business. They had previously been helped by Bernard's younger brother, Geoff, but he had left to go into the army, so Bernard really had no choice if he wished to develop the business. It also needed to be put on a more formal footing, so on 19 March 1954 Ashley Mountney Ltd. was formed.[10]

It soon became apparent that it was quite impossible to run a makeshift factory from their three-room flat, so a workshop was found at 83 Cambridge Street, Pimlico. Consisting of a large and small room, it made life considerably easier and it also enabled Bernard to build a continuous printing machine ('terrific Heath Robinson things'), which he did at his grandfathers engineering works in Sutton. His machine had a print table where the fabric could be securely held and printed with the screen or screens. It was then drawn under a bank of heat lamps to aid the drying process. In so cramped a space the room must have been unbearably hot. Bernard further refined and developed his machine and was able to make it semi-automatic by using compressed air. It eventually grew to be 30 feet long and could produce 200

The print table at Cambridge Street, with fabric drying beneath the arrangement of heat lamps.

to 300 yards of fabric a day. They used the small room as an office, with the alcove becoming the dye works. At the time they were using pigment dyes, which remain on the surface of the fabric rather than chemically reacting with the fibres of the fabric as reactive dyes do. These are more complex compounds and require more sophisticated finishing to fix the colour.

Bernard was the colourist and to him colours were like language; they had a rhythm and a flow.[11] The colour palette, for which they were to become famous, began to evolve here, but the fashions and tastes of the times dictated some of the colours that were used, and the scope of their printing technology brought further limitations. This colour palette consisted of around twenty colours from bright oranges and reds, to browns and subdued blues.[12] When they moved to Cambridge Street they had no fixing oven, so product had to be sent out for finishing. Accidents do happen of course and did, but for a small business trying to establish itself these losses were serious. Bernard, ever inventive, decided to build his own continuous fixing oven, which he did, although an employee recalled that it 'regularly caught fire' filling the room with fumes.[13]

One of the main reasons Bernard decided to build a fixing oven was because he had been working on a range of furnishing fabrics, and it was necessary to be able to print and finish standard piece lengths (a piece being 60 yards in those days). Looking at these furnishing fabrics today, more than fifty years later, they come as quite a surprise simply because they are so radically different from what we all popularly assume to be a quintessential Laura Ashley fabric. They are brash, bold, uncompromisingly modern (in a 1950s sense) and loud. Their names are indicative – 'Puebla', 'Bay Street', 'Plaza', 'Circuit', 'Vera Cruz' and 'Concorde' are but a few.[14] They were aimed at the contract market and many were bought and used by institutions such as hotels, universities and cruise ships. P&O, for example, commissioned fabrics

The 'dye laboratory' at Cambridge Street. Notice the screens stacked up in the corner.

for their ballrooms and dining rooms. One such fabric was a black and white design with details of Humphrey Lyttelton's jazz band – a keyboard; a drum set; fingers on the strings of a double bass or the valves of a trumpet; or a player's face. They used the idea of single panel designs on other occasions. Another design was of a horse and plough in a furrowed field, which sold particularly well in Holland and the United States, and was popular for curtains.[15]

These were bold and innovative designs, and the fabrics were soon noticed. The first mention of the Ashley's products in the press came in *House and Garden* in May 1955. They illustrated a design called 'Plaza' – jigsaw shapes on a white ground that retailed at 15*s.* a yard and came in narrow width (36 inches wide), as did most of these early designs. It was not until 1956 with the design 'Vera Cruz' that broad-width fabrics (48 inches wide) began to be produced. This design sold for 30*s.* a yard. More mentions in the press followed and the November issue of *House and Garden* again featured 'Plaza', but this time with matching wallpaper at 25*s.* 4*d.* per roll. It would seem that right from the very start, co-ordination had been a theme.

By now the company could produce between 100 and 300 yards of fabric a week. Ashley Mountney fabrics could be seen and ordered through large department stores such as Liberty's, Woollands and Heal's in London, as well as Dunns in Bromley and Hopewells in Nottingham. Smaller retailers also bought their domestic items, such as napkins and placemats, all of which sold so well they decided to add oven gloves to the range.

In 1955 the Ashleys had moved from London to East Cottage in Limpsfield Chart in Surrey. However, living in Surrey and maintaining a factory in Pimlico was becoming quite impractical. Bernard also realized that his activities were affecting the other tenants in the building. One day he called to chat to an officer in the Royal Army Medical Corps, who had the ground floor offices, and Bernard could hardly see him for the fumes created by his finishing oven.

TOP: 'Circuit', a fabric produced by Ashley Mountney Ltd. in 1954.

MIDDLE: D94 daisy print in purple.

BOTTOM: Another early daisy print, known as M50, this time a two-tone print.

OPPOSITE: 'Jazz Players', a single panel design created by Bernard for P&O.

Carts, one of a number of
single panel designs Bernard
devised to get round the
problem of registration with
his printing machine.

Cambridge Street had become far too cramped, so Bernard began searching for more space. He eventually found an old coach house at Brasted in Kent on the banks of the River Darent (although its proximity to the river was to have unforeseen consequences). At 1,200 square feet these roomy premises were ideal, so the business was relocated. In London two young artists had been employed (Brenda, the company's first full-time employee had been taken on in the autumn of 1954) but they both left and two young printers were employed in their stead. In the outlying villages Laura assembled a small team of outworkers to help with sewing hems and the like. Employing outworkers was to become an important part of the Laura Ashley philosophy. Laura felt particularly strongly that women with small children who were housebound could be helped by such employment.

Bernard perfected his printing machine at Brasted, and was able to produce between 200 and 300 yards a day. However, the machine was not able to register individual repeats, at least not with a high degree of consistency, which meant continuous pattern printing was difficult. They could produce furnishing fabrics, but really only in small lengths, and this was not ideal. What they needed was something that could be continuously printed, but as a single panel design. The answer was relatively simple: tea towels. Bernard found an old theatre playbill, which had a good bold typeface and simple pattern, and had a go at printing it. He found that any printing flaws only added to the quaintness of the design, so they began printing them as tea towels. At first this was thought of as a sideline, and Bernard remarked, 'I thought tea towels were very degrading', so he used Laura's name on the label instead of his own (hitherto fabrics had sold either under the Ashley Mountney name or more often as Bernard Ashley). So it became Laura Ashley and has remained so ever since.[16]

The tea towels sold like the proverbial hot cakes. Scouring Charing Cross Road they began to expand the number of designs, using Victorian or Georgian theatre

TOP: A single panel neo-classical design printed up as a tablecloth, mid-1950s.

ABOVE: Laura standing in front of a hanging in the same design in the showroom at Old Burlington Street.

bills or engravings taken from Victorian books. Some were printed on cotton and some on linen, and they retailed at 2*s*. 6*d*. or 4*s*. 11*d*. respectively. One tea towel (or more correctly a glass cloth) titled 'Anyone for washing up' was featured in *House and Garden* in April 1961. It sold for 6*s*. each. A small piece in the *Evening Standard* in May 1960 mentioned 'A two-penny stamp' blown up to twenty times life size. 'Instructions on how to cook rich gravy' was another design, and yet another was 'Where to see the feats put on by performing fleas'.[17] One of the best-sellers was a theatre bill for the new season at the Adelphi Theatre on 7 October 1822, 'when will be reproduced the Burletta *Tom and Jerry* or *Life in London*, of which so many distorted shadows have appeared'. They sold in a number of major department stores, and were soon spotted by overseas buyers. Eventually they could be purchased in Metz in Amsterdam, Au Printemps in Paris, Myers in Australia and Bloomingdales in New York. They even won an award for good design at the Sacramento Trade Fair in California.

This success was due to the determination of Laura and Bernard. One year, when business was particularly slow, they filled the battered old van with tea towels and set off the length and breadth of the country selling them, often sleeping overnight in the van. Such activities were not without incident. Returning from one such foray they encountered thick fog, making driving hazardous, so they pulled over in what they thought was a lay-by. They were woken early next morning by a crowd of people and soon discovered they had pulled into a bus stop and were surrounded by inquisitive early morning shift workers. Needless to say they were soon on their way back to Limpsfield.[18]

Such dedication and hard work built the company. The turnover doubled from £2,000 in 1955, and doubled again to over £8,000 by 1960. In 1958 they opened a showroom and London office in the basement of 9 Old Burlington Street. Bernard hung the basement hallway with lengths of fabric, and in the main room had displays of their various products. He had even created a series of single panel prints which made ideal wall hangings. The company carried no stock, so everything was printed to order, a position that had advantages as well as disadvantages. In September 1958 a disastrous storm caused the River Darent to burst its banks, flooding the coach house to a depth of 3 feet. Serious as this event was, had the company carried stock it would undoubtedly have been the ruin of them.

Laura at Old Burlington Street, the London showroom. The bolts of fabric are some of the modernist designs they then produced.

ADELPHI
THEATRE, STRAND,

THE extraordinary Success of the last Season at this Theatre, a Success totally unprecedented in Theatrical History, renders it a Duty incumbent on the Proprietors, in announcing the Commencement of a NEW SEASON, to shew that they have not been unmindful of the Encouragement bestowed by their generous Patrons, on their past Endeavours, but have sought, by the Engagement of a NUMEROUS COMPANY of PERFORMERS, of established Merit (comprising all their old favorite and many others, from the Theatres Royal) and in the Provision of a FUND of STRIKING NOVELTY, with a respectful Attention to the Wishes of the Public in every particular, to merit the unexampled Favors they have received: it is therefore with the most grateful Pleasure they announce to the NOBILITY, GENTRY, and the PUBLIC in general, that this Theatre

WILL OPEN
FOR THE WINTER SEASON,
On MONDAY, Oct. 7, 1822,

When will be RE-PRODUCED, to gratify the numerous Persons who were unable to procure Admission last Season, the ORIGINAL FAR-FAMED BURLETTA of

Tom & Jerry!
Or, LIFE in LONDON!
Of which so many DISTORTED SHADOWS have appeared.

During the Space of **93** successive Nights last Season, nearly 200,000 Persons bore Testimony to the Merits of this celebrated Piece; and its triumphal Career was then only interrupted by the necessary Closure of the House, conformably to the License of the Theatre.

In this Piece, which will be Re-produced under the immediate Revision of the Author, with NEW DRESSES, DECORATIONS, &c. an *Entirely New Grand Medley Overture and Entr'Acts Symphonies, composed expressly for the Occasion, by Mr.G.HERBERT,*

Messrs. WRENCH, WILKINSON, REEVE, PAULO, and WALBOURN, Mrs. WAYLETT, and Mrs. BAKER,

Will sustain their Original Characters of Tom, Jerry, Logic, Billy Waters, Dusty Bob, Kate, and Sue.

To which will be added, for the **FIRST TIME**, an entirely NEW FARCICAL BURLETTA, called the

New Marriage Act,
FULL PARTICULARS OF WHICH WILL BE SHORTLY ANNOUNCED.

PRINCIPAL PERFORMERS ALREADY ENGAGED.
Mr. LEE, Mr. WRENCH, Mr. WILKINSON, Mr. JOHN REEVE,
Mr. OXBERRY, *from the Theatre Royal, Haymarket,*
Mr. ELLIOTT, Mr. KEELEY, Mr. PAULO, Mr. WALBOURN,
Mr. SALTER, *from the Theatre Royal, English Opera House,*
Mr. BUCKINGHAM, Mr. St. ALBIN, Mr. W. KIRBY, Mr. DALY,
Mr. ROSS (*his first Appearance at this Theatre,*)
Mrs. WAYLETT,   Mrs. BAKER,
Miss WALPOLE, *from the Theatre Royal, Covent Garden,*
Miss PITT, Miss E. PITT, Miss JANE SIMPSON, Mrs. DALY, &c.
Leader of the Band, Mr. PARNELL.   Ballet Master, Mr. St. ALBIN.   Stage Manager, Mr. LEE.

The WARDROBE under the Superintendence of Mr. and Miss GODBEE.
The SCENIC DEPARTMENT by Mr. FRANKLIN, and Assistants, to which the Proprietors, will, in a forthcoming Novelty, be able to add the powerful Talents of Mr. WILSON.
The INTERIOR of the HOUSE has been beautified with additional Ventilators; the ORCHESTRA considerably augmented, and every Arrangement made that can conduce to the Comfort and Gratification of the Audience.
The BOX OFFICE open from 10 o'Clock till 4, and to prevent the Disappointments that occurred so frequently last Season, the PUBLIC are respectfully requested to be early in their Application, as no Reservation can possibly be made.
BOXES, 4s.   PIT, 2s.   GALLERY, 1s.
Doors to be opened at 6 o'Clock, and the Performance to commence at a Quarter before 7.   HALF-PRICE at Half-past 8.

Printed by W. GLINDON, No 51 RUPERT STREET, Haymarket, London.

THIS PAGE: Tom and Jerry tea towel. This was one of their best-selling designs.

OPPOSITE, TOP: Rowers' tea towel.

OPPOSITE, BELOW LEFT: Festiniog Railway souvenir tea towel.

OPPOSITE, BELOW RIGHT: Cricketers' tea towel, produced on a coloured base cloth. Most were white cotton or linen.

FAR LEFT: A smock made from two panels with a pocket panel sewn on to form three pockets. The bold stripes were typical of the simple patterns produced at the time.

ABOVE LEFT: An early apron printed with a design similar to those used on tea towels.

ABOVE: A 1960s apron printed with a portrait originally used as a tea towel. These designs were relatively easy to print.

BOTTOM LEFT: A patterned apron – due to the poor definition of the printing this was a 'second'. At the time Bernard's printing machine had not been perfected.

FASHION
ICON

L aura and Bernard Ashley never set out to be involved in the fashion business: rather the company was a print house that became partly a fashion house. Chance played a part in this development. Their original product lines – napkins, placemats and tea towels – all sold well, and this prompted the development of another line. Laura's grandmother had an array of aprons for various household tasks. Laura remembered: 'When I was a child in Wales, there were different aprons for different tasks: a black apron for cleaning the grates; a green apron for washing and scrubbing; and then best of all the white starched ones (with matching caps) for cooking.' This proliferation of aprons might sound excessive, but Laura's great-aunts had all been in service in London in rather grand houses, and having a different apron for a different task would have been entirely characteristic in such households.

In 1959 Laura decided to produce a gardening apron, which was soon followed by a gardening smock. These smocks proved an instant hit, and were still being produced ten years later when they were featured in *The Sunday Times*.[1] They were made from cotton drill, a heavyweight fabric much used by the army, and not all that dissimilar to denim, although not often used in fashion at the time. The smocks were very simple garments, each with a front and back panel sewn together, to which was added a pocket panel, sewn to create three kangaroo pockets. They were approximately knee length, sleeveless of course, and usually produced in a striped print – orange/red and blue/green being amongst the most popular of the nine different combinations Bernard devised. Priced at 29*s*. 6*d*. or 39*s*. 6*d*. depending on the fabric quality and the print design, they sold exceptionally well to Home Counties ladies – Tenterden in Kent and Horsham in West Sussex being among the best outlets – but they were also bought by younger women, who turned them into fashion garments. The smock's design was in many ways strikingly similar to that of the sack dress, a simple loose-style dress with a rounded neck and diagonal pockets produced by Balenciaga in his 1959 collection.[2]

It was also in 1959 that the company began to produce its first flower motifs, for which they were subsequently to become famous. Again printing technology dictated

BELOW: Viv Albertine (of The Slits) with Paul Simonon (of The Clash). She is wearing a late 1960s smock dress with a wide yoke collar. One of Jane Ashley's distinctive publicity photographs.

RIGHT: Basic dress in green daisy print D94, the first floral print. It was made in four panels.

BELOW RIGHT: A smock, in a small sprig print with a stand-up neck and button-cuffed sleeves as sold in Pelham Street in the late 1960s. The print is S771, a small bud pattern.

LEFT: Balenciaga's sack dress from his 1959 collection, which was remarkably similar to the smocks that the Ashleys produced.

TOP: A very early photograph used in an advert in *Vogue* on 1 April 1970. Wide sleeves with gathered elbows, lace trim and gathered bodice were typical of the detailing used at the time. The print is again S771.

the form of the design, in this case a very simple daisy with four petals printed in a single colour on a coloured base fabric. The humble daisy was a sort of emblem of the 1960s; Mary Quant used one as her logo. Known as D94 the Ashleys' daisy came in a myriad of bright primary tones, some not a little garish, and was ideal for aprons. Another print was a bold yellow with deeper yellow daisies overprinted. Bernard used this idea in other colours – two shades of scarlet red, emerald green and bright blue.

Laura was keen to have a shop and her chance came when the family moved to Machynlleth in mid-Wales in 1960 and bought three small cottages, one of which was a tiny shop. This first venture into retailing proved to be a success. They sold all sorts of locally produced things such as honey and walking sticks, together with their own printed products – neck scarves, tablemats, napkins and the like – it was, a family friend who met them while they lived here said, 'their green wellie period'.[3] There was just enough space at the back of the shop to accommodate a woman with a sewing machine, which gave Laura the opportunity to experiment with other dress designs. Ceinwen Edwards, who had done an apprenticeship in a ladies underwear factory, was delighted to be offered a job with the Ashleys, and had just the skills they needed.[4] Working together, Ceinwen and Laura were gradually able to develop their own patterns rather than rely on those commercially available. One product they developed together was a collarless shirt, often called a 'granddad' shirt, which they probably adapted from a commercially made shirt. It was bought by students from Aberystwyth University who often wore them with belts, reminiscent of nineteenth-century Russian peasants. Laura also developed a simple Welsh costume in flannel for children, which took just fifteen minutes to make, so little girls could sit and wait while the garment was miraculously created.[5]

Naturally Laura's interest in dress design spread by local gossip, and one day two elderly ladies appeared at the door and presented Laura with an eighteenth-century ball gown.

She displayed it in the shop window, and the generous gift prompted her to experiment with making a number of different long dresses to display alongside it. These long dresses were bought by locals and visitors alike and their simple design – which meant they were relatively easy to make – made them suitable for a variety of occasions and uses from parties and even weddings to beach dresses.

In 1961 Bernard moved the factory from Brasted in Kent to the old Tybrith social club in Carno, about 15 miles from Machynlleth. He had met a local councillor, Francis Thomas, at the pub and asked him if there were any premises he could turn into a factory. Francis knew the ideal place.

At 3,000 square feet the old social club was slightly more than double the space of the coach house at Brasted. The people of Carno – it had a population of about four hundred at the time – were shrewd enough to grasp immediately what the Ashleys were trying to do and how it might benefit them and the area, so, as Bernard put it, 'they decided to join in', thus ensuring the success of the business. Today it is perhaps difficult to appreciate just how important the arrival of the Ashleys was to the local community. It meant, as Bernard noted, 'that a lot of people didn't have to leave the immediate area and go for jobs in either the new towns around here or go to the Midlands. They would stay here. A lot of the people who work here [at Carno] have their own farms and they have long weekends – a four and a half day week – so they've got plenty of time to spend on the farm as well.'[6] In later years, as the business grew and expanded, exhausting the pool of available labour in the immediate area, the Ashleys opened satellite factories in areas with high unemployment. 'We took the work to them, the idea being to open a factory where there was a pool of labour.'[7] Garments would be cut at Carno and then trucked out to be made up, with Carno acting as the mother factory. It was an innovative and also a practical idea, but it also showed the strong altruistic feelings that were a considerable motivating factor for the Ashleys.[8]

Within five years the company had outgrown the old

social club and desperately needed more space. Bernard looked at a parcel of land in Carno, but a planning application to build a factory was refused on the grounds of access. Francis Thomas again came to the rescue by suggesting the old railway station. The granite station building (of 600 square feet) – closed in June 1965 to passenger traffic (freight trains still ran on the line) – and the old shunting shed (of 1,500 square feet), plus a little more than an acre of land, were for sale at £1,200. Bernard at first thought it much too small, but soon realized the potential and the fact that it was an almost unbelievable bargain. He bought it on 23 February 1966. With characteristic energy Bernard set to work, planning permission being considered a minor inconsequential detail, and Francis Thomas often being called upon to smooth the ruffled feathers of officialdom. By now the workforce numbered twenty-four and by calling on 'cousin whoever' they began building a 3,600-square-foot extension, as well as renovating and adapting the existing buildings. The Ashleys fostered good relations with their neighbours, and the local farmers willingly lent their tractors to help in building work. In return the Ashleys would lend their cutters to help with the sheep shearing, as the cutters had originally been sheep shearers.

Initially the Ashleys persuaded their two printers to move to Wales, but one became so homesick he left within weeks. He was soon replaced by a local man, who joined two full-time machinists and a secretary. By using a selection of fashion magazines such as *Vogue* and *Harpers Bazaar*, commercially available domestic dress patterns, and their own imaginations, Laura and her team gradually expanded the range of garments. One of their creations was what became known as the 'basic dress', which started life as a maternity dress. Extremely simple to make, it consisted of a front bodice panel, a back panel and two lower panels; it had a scooped neck and the wasted fabric was utilized to make oven gloves. The dress took just ten minutes to run up. They went on to develop shirt dresses and cotton drill skirts, and

LEFT: Wool dresses as produced in the mid-1960s. Both were based on the existing smock design.

OPPOSITE: Modified smock with a stand-up neck and three-quarter-cuffed sleeves.

these simple designs proved so popular that they were to remain in production for years.

Although the company was primarily known for its cotton dresses, as early as the winter of 1966 Laura introduced a woollen dress that basically came in two styles. Both were above the knee: one with a high V-neck bodice and another with a scooped neck. They were produced in bold geometric patterns, reflecting the era in which they were made. Perhaps one reason for this was that, aside from the small shop at Machynlleth, the Ashleys were manufacturers and sold all their products into the trade. They had to produce what their wholesale customers demanded and thought they could sell. The London showroom, which had moved in 1961 from Old

Burlington Street to a first-floor studio in Lower John Street, Soho, was their primary point of contact with the trade, but what is perhaps surprising now is that most orders were despatched via parcel post. The company had no other means of delivery, the old van they had bought for £30 when they first started the business having long since fallen to pieces.

The company's timing was opportune, as the fashion business was changing and developing at a rapid pace. Before the war there were the great couture houses such as Worth, Schiaparelli and Balenciaga in Paris, and Hartnell in London. They basically led fashionable taste, as to some extent their successors still do.[9] Their patrons were a very small and select group of wealthy people, and even today a great couture house such as Chanel will have only something like two hundred customers for its haute couture collection. Yet this tiny niche market, which is in itself quite uneconomic, drives the mass-market label and is vital to the creativity of that label. After the Second World War it was Christian Dior's 1947 collection – christened the 'New Look' by Carmel Snow, the editor-in-chief of *Harpers Bazaar* – that defined a decade and helped to dispel the gloom which hung over post-war Europe. The 'New Look' was characterized by an extravagant use of fabric; one dress consumed over 20 yards, which at the time was shockingly self-indulgent. Many of the design houses with which we are familiar today began in the 1950s and 1960s. Pierre Cardin, for example, began his fashion house in 1950 (he was expelled from the *Chambre Syndicale* in 1959 for having the temerity to launch a ready-to-wear collection for Printemps, the Parisian department store) and Yves Saint Laurent, who was head designer at Dior, founded his own fashion house in 1961.

However, a different sort of fashion was starting to emerge, not in France but in England. In October 1955 Mary Quant opened her boutique Bazaar at 138a King's Road, Chelsea. Bazaar was not a couture house: rather it was a small individual boutique business, which offered a style that was a sophisticated reflection of street fashion. Mary Quant became the high priestess of 60s fashion, but her name will be forever associated with the mini skirt.[10] Whether Mary Quant invented the mini skirt or not is a moot point (it had probably been developed by André Courrèges in Paris), but she certainly named it – actually after her favourite motorcar.[11] As the 60s progressed she evolved a style which became known as the 'Chelsea look'. Her designs were simple, clean cut and for the young (Twiggy was the archetypal model). She used cotton gabardines in bright geometric patterns, but she also used a lot of man-made fibres, as did some of her rivals. She even made skirts from the PVC used for rain macs.

Another trendsetter was Barbara Hulanicki, who opened her store Biba at 87 Abingdon Road, Kensington in September 1964. Biba sold cutting-edge fashion at mass market prices.

Barbara had originally set up Biba Postal Boutique with £30 after leaving Brighton Art College in the late 1950s. She recalled: 'We were hard-core street [fashion]: Mary Quant was more posh, and Laura was more blue blood – Sloane Ranger. Jean Muir was more "ladies who lunch", only they didn't lunch in those days.'[12] Her first major success came in May 1964 when she offered a pink gingham dress at under £3 to readers of the *Daily Mirror*.[13] Within the first day she had 4,000 orders and she eventually sold 17,000 dresses. The shop did just as well and within five years she had moved to larger premises in Kensington Church Street, and subsequently moved again to the old Derry & Toms department store building on Kensington High Street, opening as Big Biba in September 1973.

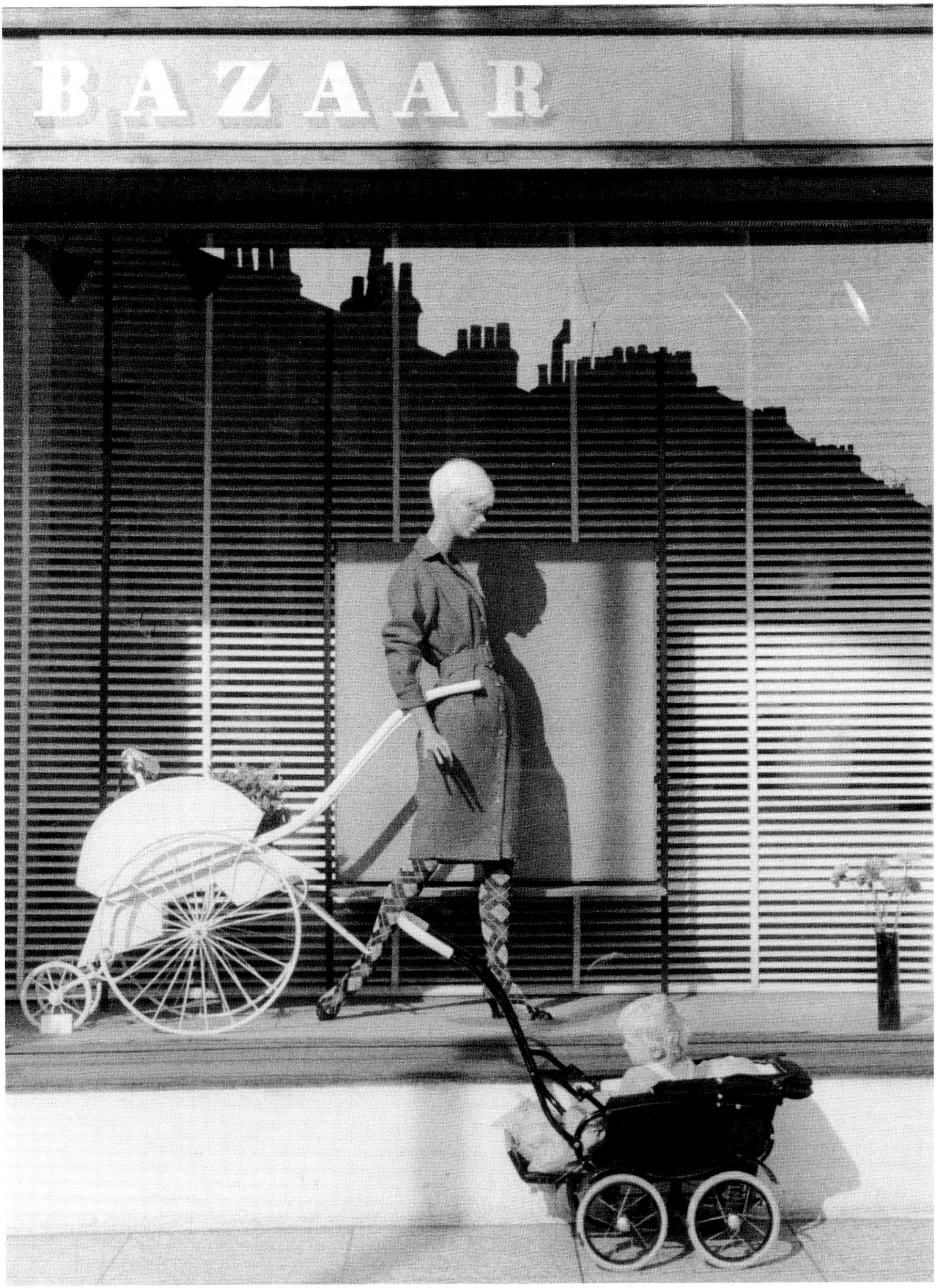
BAZAAR

Ossie Clark was perhaps the other dominant figure from the late 1960s and although he was involved in retail fashion, he was really a *couturier*, and an immensely gifted one at that.[14] At school he had studied architecture and this gave him a unique understanding of scale and proportion, which he went on to apply to his clothes. After studying at the Royal College of Art (he graduated in 1965 with a first-class degree) he began designing for Alice Pollock's shop Quorum, which was saved from bankruptcy in 1968 by the fashion house Radley. Ossie understood not only scale and proportion, but also female anatomy and how the body moved. He knew almost instinctively how to cut and to construct his garments to fit beautifully. His tailoring was always superb and it was this that made his clothes so special.

A rather forgotten figure from the period was John Bates, who founded Jean Varon in 1959. Bates too was innovative, using modern fabrics, and he pushed at the conventions, for instance by using undergarments as outerwear. He was also a perceptive observer of the scene, remarking 'a lot of fashion is in the air and everybody plucks it out of the air at the same time. But I do think that sensitivity to fashion's mood is a very English thing.'[15] It was certainly in the air in Wales. Laura never set out to compete with, nor to emulate Mary Quant, Jean Muir or Barbara Hulanicki, but she did have a clear idea of where she stood in contemporary fashion – 'I always think I'm the country one and she's [Mary Quant] the town one. She's marvellously urban in the way that Barbara Hulanicki was; marvellously, excitingly urban whereas I've never lived in the city, or if I've had to live in a city I've still got my roots in the country. It's a completely different scene altogether for me.'[16]

Bernard began to find that pandering to wholesale customers wasn't all that much fun, and he also began to find them over cautious and very picky. But having built up more than five hundred accounts he felt he could not afford to alienate them, or to ditch them and go straight into retailing. Another major problem with wholesale customers was the

TOP: Pelham Street, the Ashleys' first London shop in South Kensington, which opened in June 1968.

ABOVE: The interior of Pelham Street, which was very simply and cheaply fitted out.

RIGHT: 'Three Emmas', the second advert Bernard devised, featuring their youngest daughter, Emma.

length of time it took some of them to settle their accounts. One well-known department store only settled every six months, and this played havoc with the cash flow of a small under-capitalized business like the Ashleys'.[17] After retailing in a very modest way at Machynlleth, a subsequent partnership venture in London – Boys on Knightsbridge Green – had not been a success and Bernard had been very lucky to escape virtually unscathed.[18] This had put him off retailing, although not entirely. One of his wholesale customers was a small couture designer in Paris and he became intrigued by the man's business: 'I was in his shop, which is a tiny shop about 1,500 square feet on the Left Bank in Paris in Saint Germain. He had a turnover of £5,000 a week, which at that time was incredible. So I said to him one day, "How the heck do you do it?" His answer was quite simple: "I sit in the back of my shop and I watch all the customers coming in." Of course what he was doing was observing and noticing their reactions to the goods offered and by doing this he stayed in close touch with the prevailing mood on the street.' When Bernard related this story to Laura her answer was equally simple: 'Open a shop.'

Bernard protested that they really didn't have the money to do that. Laura had an answer to that too: 'Put it on a barrow'![19] He was having none of it, but two years later he finally gave in and agreed to open the first Laura Ashley shop.

After some searching, they eventually found a small shop at 23 Pelham Street, South Kensington. Opened in June 1968, the shop was not a huge success – initially at any rate. A small piece appeared in *The Times* on 24 June 1968 announcing its opening. It stocked 'gaily patterned dresses for mothers and daughters, with matching aprons, oven gloves, mats and household textiles' and all at reasonable prices. An adult dress was just £1 19s. 6d. – they shrewdly kept the price point just below £2; and a child's dress was £1 4s.[20] Despite the prices and favourable press comment, the first six months were a disappointment, with turnover of about £300 a week, which was barely sufficient to make the shop profitable. It was then that Bernard decided to use advertising, which they had always been against. He engaged a photographer to photograph a model wearing a maxi dress in corduroy with a high neck, tucks along the bodice and a

I always have to wear
my sister's
cast offs. Actually,
she really does cast off
quite a lot
because
she's always getting
new
Laura Ashley
dresses
But now Mummy
has got

the message . . . .
and she's buying
my size
and her size
too.
The
grown up
cast off is
£5 - 5 - 0
and mine is
75/-. My name
is Emma Ashley

LAURA ASHLEY SHOPS - SOUTH KENSINGTON   GROWN UPS **157 Fulham Road SW3**   KIDS **23 Pelham St SW7**

OPPOSITE: Emma and Sara Freeman, taken by Bernard in 1968.

TOP: A picnic, typical of the lifestyle the company projected. From left, Sara, Nick, Robina, Laurel and 'GC'.

FAR LEFT: A multi-coloured tiered skirt from the 1970s.

LEFT: A long dress made in plain fabric with plain detailing.

Mother's dress, £3 5s. 6d., Oven glove, 8s., Child's plain dress £1 4s. and printed apron 12s. All from Laura Ashley, 23 Pelham Street, London, S.W.7.

DRAWING BY JUDY MARKHAM

Laura Ashley is doing for Wales what Donald Davies has done for Ireland. The aprons and house dresses which she used to make in printed cotton on her kitchen table in Machynlleth, Wales, are exported to the United States and Switzerland.

Her original, individual, gaily patterned dresses for mothers and daughters, with matching aprons, oven gloves, mats and household textiles now have a London home at 23 Pelham Street, London, S.W.7. The styles and patterns are limited, but the shop is speckled with colour and the prices, from £1 19s. 6d for adult dresses and from £1 4s. for children's, should ensure Laura Ashley's success and keep this summer's new factory busy for many seasons to come.

A small piece from *The Times* of 24 June 1968 about the new shop in Pelham Street, South Kensington.

full skirt with a wide frill, which sold for a mere 6 guineas. 'I took 100 posters on the London Underground and advertised one dress. Three days later our turnover had gone up 300 per cent: two months later it had gone up 3,000 per cent. We were in the retailing business.'[21] They never looked back.

Opening the shop in South Kensington also coincided with developments in the products. Bernard explained: 'I said to my wife one day, "Listen, you know what we want in our business. We want to sell cloth, because I'm a textile printer. Why the heck don't we do a long dress, because women have worn long dresses for hundreds of years, and that will use 6 or 7 yards of my fabric."' Actually the first long dress used 10 yards of fabric. This meant that when people tried to copy it, as many did, they couldn't produce the effect for the same cost, so copies ended up being more expensive than the originals. Bernard observed: 'That was our first lesson in verticality, because we could sling it all together, we were producing the fabric at a very low cost and we could afford to use 10 yards.'[22] Becoming a vertical company gave them greater control, but very early on they recognized the importance of the price: 'It's very much part of our design philosophy to always have the price in hand with the design, and in order to achieve this we always try to manufacture as much of the product as we can. In textiles we take over from the loom and do every other process after that right up to where we actually take the cash across the counter.'[23] This meant they knew exactly what did and what did not sell, and even which colours were popular and which were not. Manufacturing product locally was not uncommon then, whereas today it would be uneconomic, so most of it is done in far-flung parts of the world, then it was very difficult to control production thousands of miles away. It was, however, unusual to be both retailer and manufacturer.

Once the shop was established and had a name, customers would call to see what was new, and on numerous occasions the small shop became so crowded that they were forced to lock customers out. At the time they didn't do collections: there was no point, as they were not showing to the trade. They produced new things virtually every week, a fact customers soon latched on to. The designers worked to very tight timescales: from the conception of a new dress design to having dresses on sale in the shop took a mere two and a half weeks.[24]

A little over a year later, in 1969, they opened yet another shop, this time in Shrewsbury, selling the tiny shop at Machynlleth. Again sales were initially disappointing, but the appointment of Jean Revers as manageress transformed the situation. At the same time an extension was built at Carno to house two Stork printers, both bought second-hand. These very accurate machines could produce 35,000 metres of fabric a week and could also print in six colours. This brought new possibilities.

All these events meant that the company had an opportunity to move away from the geometric patterns that had characterized the sixties to more floral prints with more complex colour combinations. Even after annexing the adjoining shop, Pelham Street proved to be too small, so in May 1970 they opened a new shop at 157 Fulham Road. As a condition of the lease the façade had to be green marble, and this elegant colour combination – green and cream – has remained the company's signature ever since. Veronica Papworth, writing in the *Sunday Express* described it as 'one of the liveliest shops in London – high, wide, airy with whitewashed walls, polished floors …'. It was an instant success. The company had taken on a designer, Jacqui Smale, fresh out of the Royal College of Art. She proved to be a great designer and created many of the original basic designs. Later her name appeared on specific products, which were labelled the 'Jacqui Smale's Custom collection', although it was soon realized that crediting a designer diluted the brand's image and ever after all the designers who worked for the company were to remain anonymous. After Jacki Smale left most of the new designs were the work of Tim Gardner, who worked freelance, but the company needed an in-

Laura Ashley New Shop opens May 4th at 157 Fulham Road, S.W.3, with the summer collection (and Jacqui Smale's Custom collection) All in Laura Ashley fabrics printed and dyed in Wales. Children's clothes and a new fabrics shop will be at 23 Pelham Street, S.W.7. South Kensington Station for both shops.

Advert for the new shop in Fulham Road. Also advertised, 'Jacqui Smale's Custom collection'. After Jacqui left all the designers were to remain anonymous.

house designer. The manageress of the Pelham Street shop, Surapee Karnasuta had a friend, Sonny Vipatasilpin, who had been the foremost classical dance teacher in Thailand. She had no real experience of fashion designing, save for some theatre design. The Ashleys appointed her chief designer. It was a daring and an imaginative idea, but it was also rather shrewd. Sonny had a grasp of the 'English romantic' look that probably no native could have had. It was Sonny who in the years ahead created many of the best-selling garments, simply because she understood what women wanted to buy. Laura observed: 'Many would-be designers have the idea that they only want to do their own thing, or create works of art. In my opinion, a work of art goes on a *wall* – not on a woman! It's suicide to design for yourself; we design only for the customer, to meet her tastes. You need to have a firm idea of your aims.'[25]

OPPOSITE LEFT: A Victorian-style dress, probably from the early 1970s, with lace trimming. The print is S19 and is similar to the furnishing fabric pattern launched in 1972.

OPPOSITE RIGHT: Lucy and Tim at Rhydoldog, taken in 1976.

LEFT: A patchwork dress, probably produced in the early 1970s.

RIGHT: A typical Empire-style dress with a high waistline, pin-tucked bodice panel and tiered frilled sleeve. The print is S112.

Laura Ashley Winter 74

LCT1
LSK82 (D)

LCT2
LSK75 (D)

MC 72
MSK 76

MC 74
MSK 66

MC75
MSK 84 (D)

MC79
+ MSK 66

C5.

C3.

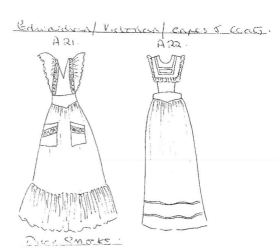

Edwardian/ Victorian/ capes & coats.

A 21.

A 22.

Dress Smocks

ABOVE: Coats, capes and smocks from the Winter 1974 collection.

RIGHT: Laura's sketch and instructions for dresses for the Spring 1974 collection.

OPPOSITE TOP: Winter 1974, sketches for dresses. This shows the diversity of the designs then available.

OPPOSITE BELOW: Sketches for blouses from the same collection.

Spring 1974.

Thin strappy dress, long,
bias skirt.
Same with knee length
skirt.

Same rough peasant cotton
with tiny sprigged
prints.
More like later Western
clothes. Sprigged ~~short~~
blouse with white collar
+ cuffs.
Shirt dress with peter
pan collar in white,
lowish,

more like   Dr, Finlays
1930 Scottish

Laura Ashley Winter 74 Collection.

L108 Elizabethan dress.   L99   L100   L102   L121   L104   L188

We have added some new styles and free sheet

Special occasion dress or Ball dress.

L123   L155   N49   L50   L185   L195

Simple Victorian dress.
Kate Greenaway type dress.
Special Laura Ashley Wedding dresses

Victorian/low Victorian
Neck Bustle   Highneck Bustle.

Special Edwardian
Dress with train.

Laura Ashley Winter 74 Collection

B40   B49   B114   B115   B116   B117   B113

B87   B102   B103   B109   B108   B107   B91

B105   B106

Victorian/Edwardian and simple blouses White lawn/Print Plain cotton

S271 swan print dress
with a V-neck and a high
pin-tucked waist.

Laura was adamant that the most important point about any brand was the emotion behind it; that was its core, its intellectual roots. In Laura's case it was very much the country.[26] In a way it had shades of Jane Austen – small country manors and country fashions. Laura was, as she recalled years later, latching onto another important emotion: nostalgia. 'We find anything with a nostalgia about it goes: it's always a winner. I think people want to find a security at home. They're not particularly – as you notice – [clothes] for making a splash in a dramatic place; they're simple garments to wear at home, and when you get home perhaps you need the security of nostalgia.'[27]

Laura saw herself as selling a dream of an idealized country life during that long golden afternoon that was Edwardian England. She remarked: 'I think that in England at the turn of the century … people in quite a comfortable way … had a wonderful life, because they made the most of it. I think it all got rather broken up with the First World War, and we need to get back to that again.'[28] Of course the Edwardian age did not exactly mirror the reign of King Edward VII, but he and Queen Alexandra had become fashion leaders from the late 1860s when they were Prince and Princess of Wales, and part of what was known as the Marlborough House set, named after their London home. Queen Alexandra was a great beauty and her style was much admired.

Fashion changed markedly in the 1890s, when the bustle disappeared and day dresses gradually adopted a more tailored silhouette – from a hand-span waist the skirt would flare smoothly over the hips, falling to a broad hemline. The French christened the look 'La Belle Époque' and it continued until the advent of war in 1914. It was satirised by the American artist Charles Dana Gibson in his image 'The New Woman', and the 'Gibson Girl' look in turn became very fashionable. Following the outbreak of war in 1914 fashion changed again, perhaps most notably apparent in the hemline. Many of the designs prevalent throughout the war and into the early 1920s could be comfortably worn

OPPOSITE, FROM TOP TO BOTTOM:

A red dress with a rounded neck and cuffed elbow sleeves. The skirt was tiered with ruched edging.

A three-quarter-length smock dress with ruched pockets.

A green dress with buttoned bodice, long puffed sleeves and button cuffs.

A plain white dress in seersucker, with lace inserts and trim and pin-tucked bodice.

THIS PAGE: A group by a barn. Laura's daughter Jane became the company's photographer and this is typical of her style. Nick Ashley is sitting in the hay door, with Laurel, Robina, Sara and 'GC' standing below.

OPPOSITE: Sara in a pin-tuck blouse with lace trim. It was blouses in this style, basically Victorian and Edwardian designs, for which the company became famous. This picture was taken in 1973.

BELOW LEFT: Laura's sketch for a long overblouse. Laura couldn't really draw and so almost no sketches by her survive.

BELOW RIGHT: Design for blouse B90 dated 2 October 1973, by Sonny Vipatasilpin.

BOTTOM: The B90 blouse as produced.

RIGHT: The B49 Mexican-style blouse from *The Sunday Times* advert, styled by the newspaper in a more overtly raunchy way than was usually the case with Laura Ashley products.

FAR RIGHT: The B49 blouse in a rather more demure publicity photograph. This was styled by the company.

even today, whereas those from the high Edwardian period would be rather inappropriate. But for Laura the whole period offered a rich source from which she drew, ever refining, adapting and interpreting.

Laura actually had no design experience or formal training; indeed as Bernard pointed out, 'She's not a designer: she's a critic. It's her critical faculty which is her strength, and also being able to see things all the time from a critical angle. She's always getting a trend before it arrives almost and then we just follow up and exploit it.'[29] Very early on Laura shrewdly identified her customer. She understood that you couldn't possibly appeal to all of the people all of the time: you just needed to be able to appeal to some of them some of the time. In any case, there would always be sections of the public she couldn't understand or relate to, so she just cut them from her thinking. 'I actually studied what people really wanted basically … [and I] gave them what they were looking for. There are always areas in a market that are missing and we fill those areas. We don't just design freely we look for a loophole.'[30]

In some ways, if Mary Quant had been the 1960s fashion revolutionary, Laura led the 1970s counter-revolution. She recognized that the majority of women had no desire to wear mini skirts – in reality few women could convincingly wear these garments – and the next fad for hot pants was equally as absurd. Laura gave them an alternative look,

which all women, regardless of their figures, could be happy to wear. She neatly summed it up by often reminding her staff, 'now remember we're in the camouflage business'.[31] The maxi dress, which they advertised on the Underground, was an example of this thinking. With the popularity of the maxi dress, its 'Edwardianization' seemed to be a logical development. However, this development didn't come out of nowhere. Around the same time there were a number of popular costume dramas on the television. *The Forsyte Saga*, screened initially between January and July 1967 on BBC2 and then repeated on BBC1 the following year, was a brilliant adaptation of John Galsworthy's Edwardian and later novels, and was probably the most famous. *Upstairs Downstairs*, made and screened on ITV from 1971, was yet another.[32] The effect was repeated again in 1981 when ITV adapted Evelyn Waugh's classic novel *Brideshead Revisited*, which spawned a fashion for 1920s and 1930s dress, or what was known as the 'Brideshead look'. The Ashleys had already produced a 1920s dress with pleats in 1973, which at the time was a marked departure for them.

These Edwardian costume dramas of course had an effect on fashion, but Laura might also have been influenced by her childhood and her recollections of her grandmother. Another influence, possibly subconscious, might have been the hippie look that came to dominate fashion in the latter part of the 1960s. Originating in San Francisco in the 'summer of love' in 1967, it was anti many things, including, ironically, prevailing fashion, and the young sought inspiration from past times and different lands. It was both 'ethnic' and also 'retro'.

In January 1970 the Paris collections all emphasized long skirts, a look which was soon christened the 'midi' – simply because the hemline fell to the mid-calf. What became the quintessential Laura Ashley style developed within this trend and it developed rapidly. The style might seem Victorian or Edwardian, but it was also hugely influenced by the Empire style, prevalent in the first quarter of the nineteenth century, which was itself influenced by the styles of dress from

2171

Classic Edwardian evening dress with pebble skirt in dark printed cotton

Laura Ashley Winter Collection

76

LEFT: An Edwardian evening dress in print B1623, known as 'Almond Blossom', to the design sketch shown right.

TOP RIGHT: Sketch for an Edwardian evening dress.

BOTTOM RIGHT: Sketch design for the Edwardian-style cape coat with a button front and tie.

BELOW: Edwardian cape coat in tan cord. The design was known as C5.

long cord cape coat.

2183

80

LEFT TOP: The 'zig-zag' twin set – skirt and jacket.

LEFT MIDDLE: A high-necked blouse with a frill over the bust. Worn with an Edwardian-style 'zig-zag' skirt.

LEFT BOTTOM: A six-tiered and frilled dress with bonnet.

ABOVE: Edwardian-style wedding dress from the Winter 1974 collection.

LEFT: Sketch design for a long Edwardian-style jacket with braid trim and a 'zig-zag' braided skirt.

Edwardian long corduroy Jacket
Braid trim

Ancient Greece and Rome.[33] Such dresses created a distinctive silhouette – closely fitted to the torso just under the bust, and falling loosely below. It was a fortuitous development as the printed cotton the Ashleys produced was ideally suited to this silhouette.

In essence the style may have been remarkably simple, but it was open to myriad small nuances. A characteristic of Empire-designed dresses was the high waistline, with the skirt sometimes being tiered, or frilled. The depth of any tier, and the number of such tiers, or frills, could vary from 4 inches to as many as 15 inches. The frills were all added by hand, the machinist learning quite quickly how fast to feed in the frill so it appeared to be even. There were considerable variations: for example, the breast panel might be pin-tucked, or trimmed in some way, perhaps with lace. Sleeves were another area that showed variation. The company became famous for its 'leg of mutton' sleeves, narrow at the wrist and wide at the shoulder. Sometimes they would be quite plain, with a simple button cuff, but they could also be elaborate, with frills and lace trims. Puff sleeves were yet another style frequently used, as were cap sleeves.

Although the company became known for its cotton dresses in a multitude of prints, the range of garments was far more extensive than this and they experimented with many different designs. One dress which went into production was based on Elizabethan designs with a boned stomacher and a skirt formed over a back roll.[34] Such a dress in A5 'Sweet Rocket' print survives in the archive and may have formed part of the 'Medieval collection', which was produced in 1970. Another early dress, the L64, which had a lot of pin-tucks, was worn by the dancers Pan's People on the BBC pop music programme *Top of the Pops*.[35] The company also produced a long shirt-waisted crocheted dress; knickerbockers with matching waistcoats; capes, cloaks and coats with matching accessories such as mob-caps; sun hats and of course scarves. Its Victorian nightdesses in a range of styles became classics. In the winter of 1970 it sold one – described as 'tucked and

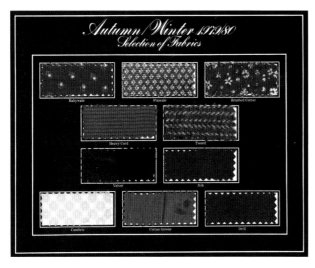

lacy gown and mob cap' – in silk for 7 guineas or in cotton lawn for £3 15s.[36]

The company diversified into corduroy, used for skirts and jackets as well as full-length dresses. Later they began to use tweed, bought from the Cambrian Woollen Mills at Llanwrtyd Wells in mid-Wales. Not only did the use of tweed fit neatly into the business, but it is another example of the altruistic attitude the Ashleys had to business. The Cambrian Woollen Mill, run by the Royal British Legion, employed a number of disabled workers, indeed of the forty-eight workers in 1977, thirty-eight had some serious disability.[37] The company paid the market price for the tweed, but it offset some of the cost by using its charity fund, subsidizing the cost by a pound a metre. This subsidy enabled the finished product to be competitive, but the mill never knew this. The general manager recalled: 'We enjoyed an Indian Summer for a good few years. She [Laura Ashley] was a wonderful friend.'[38]

This was far from an isolated example of Laura's generosity. For all her commercial success, Laura was rather shy of using the facilities of the Victoria and Albert Museum in London and preferred instead the Museum of Costume in Bath, and later the Gallery of English Costume at Platt Hall in Manchester. The latter's collection was second only to that held by the V&A, but like most museums it was badly short of funds. Laura and her researchers photographed a number of items from the collection and by way of return she offered to copy some of the dresses in the collection for an illustrated lecture. The idea was to make four copies each of forty different dresses spanning the period 1770 to 1875, but it was soon evident that 'an illustrated lecture' was not a fitting use for all this work, so it became a theatrical production, with students of the Royal Northern College of Music and the Northern Ballet school performing six vignettes inspired by scenes from everyday life. The show was staged in Manchester on 22 and 23 June 1983. There were tangible benefits for the company, aside from increasing its profile.

Of the forty dresses copied, five were put into general production, as was a cloak. But perhaps the most enduring thing to come out of this collaboration was the book *The Fabric of Society*, written by Jane Tozer and Sarah Levitt and published by Laura Ashley Ltd. in 1983.[39] Covering many of the technical aspects of eighteenth century dress design and manufacture the book was profusely illustrated, drawing on the museum's extensive collection.

Even before the book was published Laura had handed over the day-to-day work of designer to her son Nick and to Deborah James, who was fashion co-ordinator and basically oversaw the fashion side of the business. But that is, as they say, another story.

OPPOSITE TOP: Cord coat with a hood. The small pattern used as lining may be derived from those used in Indian coats.

OPPOSITE BOTTOM: The Autumn/Winter 1979/80 fabric selection included not only cotton, but corduroy, tweed and silk.

LEFT: A copy of Mrs Taylor's dress from Platt Hall.

RIGHT: Copy of a dress from Platt Hall, Manchester. Both these dresses were put into production.

Drawing inspiration from
the company archive
contemporary designs were
created. A simple spot print
and smock dress for the
1980 Spring collection.

A trouser suit from the same collection.

OPPOSITE: Carnival, off to the ball! This extravagant creation in black silk moiré was from the 'Venetian Collection', Autumn/Winter 1982.

LEFT: Plus fours and a waistcoat in a style evocative of the 1930s, from the 'Venetian Collection'.

BELOW LEFT: A tweed suit in a 1920s style, also from the 'Venetian Collection'.

BELOW: The 'plus four' look was inspired by the Gondolier's uniform.

OPPOSITE: A tailored two-piece suit from the Spring 1984 collection, reflecting the prevailing trend towards 'power dressing'.

THIS PAGE: Diana, Princess of Wales, before her marriage, wearing a Laura Ashley skirt.

THIS PAGE: The 1980 Spring/
Summer print selection
showing the prints and
colourways popular that
season.

OPPOSITE: Paris, 1980.
Simple summer dresses
from the Spring collection.

Laura Ashley meets punk. Viv Albertine, later of The Slits, and Paul Simonon of The Clash. The unusual three-tiered dress, in printed cotton, has a halter neck and button fastening at the back.

THE VICTORIAN REVIVAL

I t is perhaps one of the ironies of the Laura Ashley story that it was the fashion side of the business that first really made the company's name, and yet this side of the business in a sense started itself. The 'home furnishings were always closer to my mothers heart', her son Nick recalled, and it is the home furnishing collections which are perhaps most associated with her name today.[1] The Laura Ashley Company was never a fashion house, nor an interior decorators for that matter, but was always primarily a print house. The company developed from neck scarves, through tea towels and into garment manufacture, but these activities were always subsidiary to their main occupation as textile printers. From the start, they produced furnishing fabric for the contract market, and these bold, modern designs sold moderately well. The main problem was in production as Bernard's Heath Robinson printer had difficulty with the registration (the pattern repeat). Gradually, garment manufacture for the wholesale market and, increasingly, for their own shops, meant that the contract furnishing fabric market was abandoned, or rather it was allowed to wither away.

In 1968 the factory was producing 5,000 metres of fabric a week, and although this was usually sufficient, there were occasions when they were short of printed fabric. This prompted them to manufacture some of the garment designs in plain white cotton, which proved a great success. In 1969 Bernard was able to buy two second-hand Stork printers for £5,500. These were considerably more accurate than his own creation, and considerably faster. Their combined output was 35,000 metres a week. They not only resulted in good definition and sharper prints, but could also print in six colours. This gave much scope to develop more complicated designs and colour combinations.

The shop at 23 Pelham Street, South Kensington, which opened in 1968, was soon bursting at the seams, so they took over the adjoining shop, number 25. Here they sold fabric by the yard. People bought the fabric not only to make their own dresses, but also to make curtains and other items of soft furnishings. The company managing director was to recall years later: 'Bernard's brainwave was to sell furnishing fabrics in the old draper's fashion. No one believed that you could sell garments and

TOP: Diana, Princess of Wales, and Bernard looking at a Buser printer at Carno.

BOTTOM: A Stork printer in the Carno factory.

fabrics alongside but he proved them wrong.'[2] This became the pattern for all subsequent Laura Ashley shops, a pattern that remains to this day.

Bernard was able to buy a Buser flatbed printing machine – the Rolls Royce of printers – in 1971 for which he paid a mere £2,000. This meant they could print in eight colours. Most of this machinery came from Courtaulds, who were rationalizing their operations, selling surplus plant quite cheaply. In addition to these printers, they also bought some other pieces of machinery such as a mangle, a 15,000 lb boiler, and a step and repeat machine, which enabled them to produce much more accurate screens.[3] In 1973 there were further investments in plant, incuding a new bleaching machine and a Stork Brabant rotary printer. This new machine, together with the existing flatbeds meant there was a production capacity of 100,000 metres a week. The Stork Brabant used circular nickel screens rather than the silk or nylon screen used by the flatbeds. It enabled multi-coloured prints to be produced, as well as 'blotch prints' – where the ground colour is printed. At the time (in 1973) 80 per cent of the prints produced were single colour with a mere 15 per cent multi-coloured. By the mid-1980s 98 per cent were multi-coloured. Buying the new printer meant that they had to expand the studio and it also meant that a more accurate step and repeat machine was needed. The rotary printer used cylindrical screens, which had a photosensitive emulsion coating. A film negative bearing the print design is wrapped around the cylinder and then exposed to ultraviolet light, developing the image and leaving its impression on the cylinder. Each colour used needed a separate cylinder. At first they produced about fifteen screens a week but by the mid-1980s this had risen to over fifty.

These investments in machinery, which boosted production capacity and improved the quality of the product, also enabled further developments to the range of fabrics that could be produced. Bernard was keen to return to the contract furnishing fabric market, and this is partly what

COME SHOPPING

Above: the Laura Ashley shops sell some of the prettiest inexpensive dresses on the fashion scene, and the business, which started life in a small shed in Wales, has grown big enough to blossom out into the furnishing field as well. Since this is a manufacturing company, with its own printing and dyeing plant and retail outlets, it is possible to sell the fabrics at a lower cost to the public. The designs shown are from the new furnishing collection: some have been newly commissioned, others are adapted from old tapestries and linens. Each of the fabrics shown above is available in three qualities: a lightweight cotton for curtaining, 50p yd.; heavy cotton, 90p yd., and cotton satin, £1·50 yd., which are suitable for curtains or loose covers. Fabrics measure 48 or 50 in. wide (with one or two exceptions), are pre-shrunk and colour-fast. Laura Ashley have made up swatches of a selection from the new range for readers of *Homes and Gardens*, and I will be happy to forward these to anyone who would like them.

ABOVE: The new range of furnishing fabrics launched in 1972.

RIGHT: S31, a late 1960s or early 1970s pattern of peacocks, probably inspired either by Arts and Crafts patterns or by Indian fabrics.

FAR RIGHT: The Edinburgh shop: a typical Laura Ashley shop interior. It was Bernard's idea to style them like old-fashioned drapers.

prompted these substantial investments. The first dedicated furnishing fabric collection was launched in 1972 and a selection of designs from the collection were featured in *House and Garden* in June of that year. They illustrated ten designs, all of which were produced in lightweight cotton, heavy cotton and cotton satin, retailing at 50p a yard, 90p a yard and £1.50 a yard, all in 48-inch-wide fabric. Some of the designs were newly commissioned, but others were adapted from old tapestries and linens. One design looks remarkably similar to a Minton floor tile, and this could indeed have been an inspiration. Another design, on an ogee pattern base, looks very much like an Arts and Crafts design and could be a copy or an adaptation of a fabric by the architect C. F. Voysey. The other fabrics illustrated in *House and Garden*, with one exception, were all fairly large-scale and intricate designs but none remained in production in 1978. The only small-scale pattern was 'Bonny Dundee' and this was featured in an article that appeared in *House Beautiful* in 1976, but it too went out of production two years later.[4] The range was far more diverse than these few examples would suggest, and complemented the smaller floral patterns used in garment production. There was a demand for these too, although they were only produced in a slightly narrower width.

Laura spent hours hunting for designs. Book endpapers were a particularly rich source, as it was quite common for Victorian books to have patterned endpapers rather than plain as is now often the case. These designs could sometimes be used as they were, or re-scaled to make them suitable for dress fabric or home furnishings. They were invariably re-coloured and in the early days Bernard acted as colourist. He 'fell in love with colour; colours have the same rhythm as words', and the ability to combine colours is just as much an art as the crafting of words and sentences. 'Colour is the most important thing in textile design.'[5] Surprisingly Bernard never considered himself 'a furnishing fabric colourist', but rather a fashion colourist.[6]

The colour palette in part reflected the spirit of the times, but the Ashleys also developed a rather subtle palette with clear singing greens, dark blues, some rather smoky in tone, with myriad plums, burgundies and pinks. One could argue that the colours reflected the landscape in which they lived, and indeed the hillsides around the family home are a never-ending and ever-changing tapestry of colour, texture and form. Laura and Bernard walked the hills almost everyday or on Aberdyfi beach (or Aberdovey beach to use its old English name), so it is inevitable that these colours were firmly fixed in their subconscious. In the early days the palette was perhaps a little more muted, again reflecting the era – and also the fact that all the colours were mixed in the same dye bucket. Sometimes, like making custard, the dye mix might go a bit lumpy, and as John Griffiths recalled: 'I even had to strain lumpy dye through ladies' nylons'.[7] This meant that no two batches of the same colour were ever identical; in fact there were considerable variations in the same colour. The colours were all earthy in tone: mushroom shades, plums and sage greens. As foreign travel increased tastes began to change. People wanted much brighter and clearer tones, reflecting a desire for a fresher atmosphere at home after two weeks spent in the bright white light of Greece or Spain. People began to light their homes more brightly, and this again influenced the appreciation of colour and tone. The Ashleys also found that different colours were more popular in different countries. Navy blue was a popular colour with the Germans and the Dutch, who also liked browns, while the French loved sapphire blues and pinks, and the Americans liked yellow.[8]

Another good source for patterns, and indeed colour combinations, was *The Grammar of Ornament*, first published in 1856. Depending upon the edition this seminal work contained 100 or 112 full-page illustrations of ornament from Chinese, Persian, Indian, Arabic and other cultures, all reproduced in colour using the then new chromolithograph process. This hugely influential book was the work of the architect and designer Owen Jones (1809–1874), and even today it remains an important reference book for designers.[9] Jones was also an interior decorator and stated that 'form without colour is like a body without a soul'. Such sentiments certainly echoed the Ashley ethos. 'Wickerwork' (also known as L571), which was in the 1978 *Home Furnishings Room Planner*, is almost a direct copy of a Chinese design illustrated on Plate LIX figure 22. Other patterns such as 'Palmetto' (F303) were inspired by elements of Egyptian ornament, and 'Mr Jones' (F381) was probably derived from medieval ornament. These were all composites drawing on elements from various designs illustrated in the book.

'Wild Clematis' (S65), one of their most enduring patterns, was derived from endpapers in a Victorian book and was open to a number of interpretations as it could be printed either as a positive or a negative pattern. Another print, 'Cottage Sprig' (P767), created in 1981, was taken from a plate in *Victorian Sheet Music Lovers* by Ronald Pearsall published by David & Charles of Newton Abbot in 1972. Yet another fabric, used only for dresses, was created from the design on an old blue and white soup tureen – a fragment of the lid survives in the archive. On one occasion Laura bought a number of old Victorian postcards from a dealer on the banks of the Seine in Paris. She thought they would make an

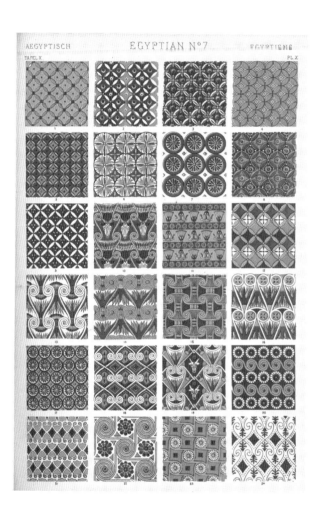

OPPOSITE: Chinese patterns from Owen Jones' famous book *The Grammar of Ornament*.

ABOVE: Egyptian patterns from Owen Jones.

TOP LEFT: 'Wickerwork' pattern L571, derived from a Chinese pattern.

BOTTOM LEFT: 'Palmetto' pattern F303.

LEFT: A fragment of a blue and white transfer-printed soup tureen from the mid-nineteenth century.

BELOW: Fabric S24, inspired by the fragment of soup tureen.

TOP: The Victorian engraving that inspired 'Cottage Sprig'.

MIDDLE: 'Cottage Sprig' pattern P767.

BOTTOM: 'Nutmeg' pattern S49, a great favourite with the public. It was designed by Brian Jones from a patchwork quilt.

attractive wallpaper for a child's room, but in the event does not seem to have been put into production. Laura was always looking for ideas and it is now difficult, with any degree of certainty, to say what the exact origin of most prints were.

Old quilts and other items of patchwork which Laura collected were a valuable source, as were the fancy coats made in India that often had very small motif designs used as lining fabric. These could be copied and sometimes re-scaled and invariably re-coloured. One member of the design team would often photocopy motifs, cut them out and then paste them onto various background colours so they could be viewed pinned to a wall and at a distance. What might seem a good combination when laid horizontally on a desk could prove otherwise when viewed vertically on a wall. The pattern could become distorted or difficult to see when viewed from a distance. Sometimes a pattern can 'walk'. For example, if you look at a letter in thick red colour, then look at a plain white surface, the same letter appears but in green. These were some of the tricks Gertrude Jekyll used in her colour combinations in the garden, and while charming in the garden they can be a disaster in decoration. Stripes, in particular, can 'walk' if the colours are too strong, which can be especially irritating after a glass of wine.

Laura described many of the designs as coming from 'my own special world of fruitful flowers, mythical animals and small geo-figurations'.[10] She had a habit of taking any pattern and flicking it back and forth, side to side, to see if it created any undesirable images. One fabric, which in some angles and lights appeared as a swastika, was rejected for obvious reasons. Some fabrics, particularly in the latter years, were created from old documents or pieces of fabric assiduously collected by Laura. In the 'Drawing Room Fabric Collection' launched in 1983 were several fabrics drawn from this collection. One, 'Venetia' (F99) was copied from Italian brocade, while 'Florentina' (F358), a pattern launched the following year, was discovered in a palazzo in Florence. A couple of the design studio staff had been sent on a

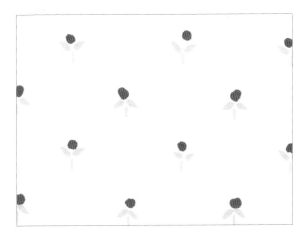

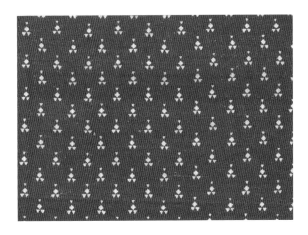

trip to Rome, Florence and Venice looking for fabrics, but France seems to have been a more fruitful hunting ground. 'Shepherds Purse' (R193) came from a document in the Musée des arts Décoratifs in Paris. Of course every other textile company was doing exactly the same thing, but Laura Ashley were seldom pipped to the post. There was one occasion when they did a charming print of lily-of-the-valley only to find someone else doing an almost identical design copied from the same original document.[11]

Regional museum collections in the United Kingdom were another fruitful hunting ground, as was the Victoria and Albert Museum in London. In those days it was possible to photograph textiles, and so easy to copy them. These days cash-strapped museums have realized the value of their collections. Historic houses were another useful source, and just five weeks before her untimely death Laura went to visit Chatsworth in Derbyshire.[12] She spent a very happy and absorbing day rummaging through cupboards and drawers behind the scenes. The Duchess recalled: 'We looked in cupboards I had never seen in the hinterland near the laundry and found some beautiful, and beautifully tied with ribbon, examples of chintzes, cottons and the rest, used over the years throughout the house and possibly other Cavendish houses.'[13] What impressed everyone at the time was that Laura 'knew exactly what was right and yet she was completely unbossy about it; she had that unerring sense, not just of good taste, but of what other people wanted.'[14] All the staff were equally impressed as they had expected a rather grand lady. When Laura arrived she 'took off her coat, put on a smock, and started work'.[15] Laura came away from Chatsworth with no less than thirty-seven documents, of which three where put into production immediately. 'Morning Tracery (F948), 'Pot-pourri' (F949) and 'Priory' (F950) were all in the 1987 catalogue and are either faithful reproductions or slight adaptations – usually the background was altered – of fabrics found at Chatsworth. Another fabric she liked very much proved impractical to reproduce because the background was

so integral to the design and was impossible to reproduce on the quality of base fabric the company used.

The Ashleys recognized that home furnishing products were a more stable sort of business than fashion, where the market is particularly fickle and changeable. In 1976 Laura remarked: 'We are moving into interior decoration much more with the success of the furnishing fabrics and wallpapers. It's just really an extension of the same lifestyle, following through from the basic concept of the garments.'[16] Laura and Bernard saw their market clearly and realized 'there will always be a market for yesterday mixed in with our style of living'.[17] It was really all about selling a dream, or as Laura put it 'selling a way of life', adding with a glint in her eye, 'British people are less neurotic than others, and probably they [foreign customers] find some of it in our products'.[18] Perhaps they did. The Ashleys were developing a market that customers had themselves created: in 1973 home furnishing products – fabrics, wallpaper, paint – made up a very small proportion of the turnover, but by 1978 it made up 48 per cent of gross sales.

In the early days the company had produced just a few co-ordinating wallpapers. 'Plaza' seems to have been one design, featured in *House and Garden* in November 1955, which was available both as a fabric and as wallpaper. The production of wallpapers then ceased and it was only in 1974 that the idea was revived. They bought a wallpaper machine (probably second-hand) and started to produce wallpapers to match the existing fabrics. At first they didn't use the right weight of paper and it took some time for them to work out

OPPOSITE TOP LEFT: 'Venetia', copied from an Italian brocade.

OPPOSITE MIDDLE LEFT: 'Florentina', a pattern found in Florence, launched in 1984.

OPPOSITE BOTTOM LEFT: 'Shepherd's Purse' pattern R193. A popular favourite,

copied from an eighteenth-century French pattern.

ABOVE: The original fabrics from Chatsworth.

RIGHT: The copies produced: 'Pot-pourri', 'Morning Tracery' and 'Priory'.

LEFT: Pattern B36 produced in 1973, a two-tone print typical of the period.

BELOW: Pattern D11, known as 'Pelican', produced in the 1960s.

RIGHT: A small bud pattern from the mid-1960s.

BOTTOM RIGHT: B45, a daisy and geometric design produced in 1973/4.

OPPOSITE: A production card from January 1977. Only three of the prints were named: R143 is 'Campion', R150 'Petite fleur' and S49 'Nutmeg'.

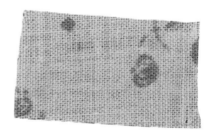

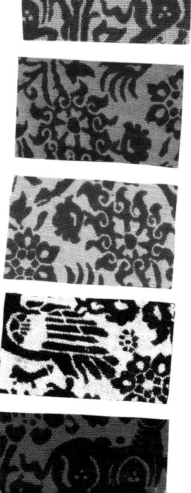

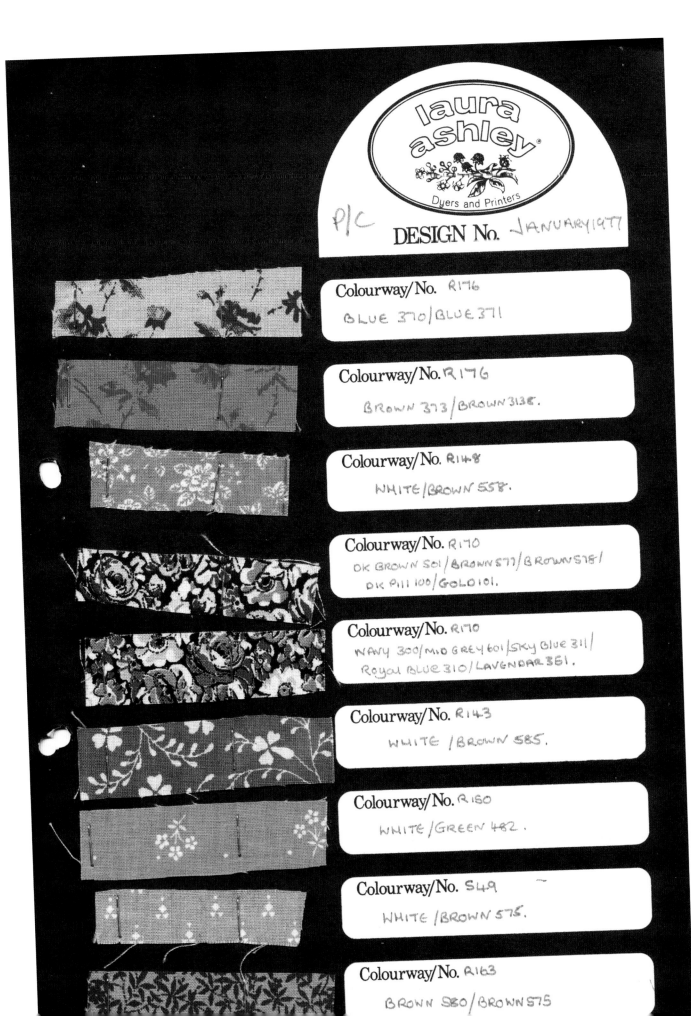

laura ashley®
Dyers and Printers

P/C

DESIGN No. JANUARY 1977

Colourway/No. R176
BLUE 370/BLUE 371

Colourway/No. R176
BROWN 373/BROWN 313B.

Colourway/No. R148
WHITE/BROWN 558.

Colourway/No. R170
DK BROWN 501/BROWN 577/BROWN 578/
DK PINK 100/GOLD 101.

Colourway/No. R170
NAVY 300/MID GREY 601/SKY BLUE 311/
ROYAL BLUE 310/LAVENDAR 361.

Colourway/No. R143
WHITE /BROWN 585.

Colourway/No. R150
WHITE/GREEN 482.

Colourway/No. S49
WHITE /BROWN 575.

Colourway/No. R163
BROWN 580/BROWN 575

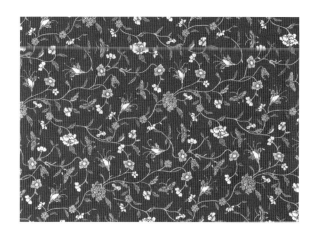

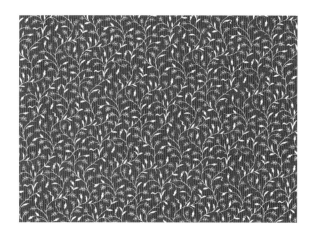

OPPOSITE: The *Home Furnishings Room Planner* from 1979 was the precursor to the popular catalogues.

ABOVE: 'Floribunda' and (bottom) 'Milfoil', both featured in the *Room Planner*.

OVERLEAF LEFT: The 1981 *Home Furnishings* catalogue.

OVERLEAF RIGHT: L571 (top), known as 'Wickerwork', as a positive and negative print. Using the same pattern in this way became hugely popular in the 1970s and 1980s. P784 (bottom) 'Wind Spray', in red on white, a more modernist design which again reflects the era, and was based on American Folk Art.

the correct amount of pressure to use. Wallpaper gradually became an important product line and by 1978 all the furnishing fabric patterns were also produced as wallpapers, although not in every colourway. In 1977 they decided to expand the range to paint and the following year they had twenty shades of emulsion and twenty-one shades of gloss paint. They further diversified, selling accessories such as cushion covers, table linens, double-sided quilted fabric and also plasticized fabric. They even sold plain ceramic lamp bases and lampshades, either plain or in one of eight different patterns, some available in different colour combinations. Ceramic wall and floor tiles in a variety of plain colours or patterns were another early line.

It was in 1978 that the Ashleys came up with another innovation: a catalogue. They had started offering mail order in 1976, and the first home furnishings catalogue was a large fold-out card, not the glossy book with which we are now so familiar. The booklet, called the *Home Furnishings Room Planner*, illustrated, at half scale, twenty-one prints plus one border design, together with twenty-one plains in furnishing cotton. The majority of prints were also available as wallpaper. None of the prints had names, and were instead identified by a letter and number code. Some, such as the L570 (later known as 'Milfoil'), a two-tone pattern, came in eight different colourways. There were only five multi-coloured prints and these were in a much more restricted range. L577 (later known as 'Floribunda'), for example, was produced in just four colourways.

The *Room Planner* proved a great success, and so in 1980 they produced a mail order catalogue in the United States. This small booklet ran to just twenty pages and advertised 'country furnishing cottons in 97 designs/colourways' and also contained many accessories such as desk furnishings – diaries and address books – and ladies dressing accessories such as trinket boxes, sewing boxes, cosmetic and travel bags. It included a small selection of garments – a couple of blouses retailing at $55 and two nightdresses. At the time the

S105 SAND/WHITE

Head Office

Carno
Powys Wales
Tel 05514 671

Showrooms

75 Lower Sloane St
London SW3

22 Rue de Grenelle
75007 Paris
Tel 544 63 04

BRITISH SHOPS

71/73 Lower Sloane Street
London SW3
Tel 01 730 1771

40 Sloane Street
London SW1
Tel 01 235 9728

10 Spittal Street
Edinburgh
Tel 031 229 9739

404 Byres Road
Glasgow
Tel 041 339 5911

12 New Bond Street
Bath Somerset
Tel 0225 60341

17 St. Mary Street
Shrewsbury Salop
Tel 0743 4744

26/27 Little Clarendon Street
Oxford
Tel 0865 52477

3/5 Dove Street
Norwich
Tel 0603 26533

17/19 Watergate Row
Chester
Tel 0244 316403

30 Great Oak Street
Llanidloes Powys Wales
Tel 05512 2828

58 Bridlesmith Gate
Nottingham Notts

1 Queens Circus
Montpellier Cheltenham

S57 CREAM/SMOKE

CONTINENTAL SHOPS

Paris

95 Avenue Raymond Poincaré
75016 Paris
Tel 704 41 73

Lyons

1 Quai Tilsitt
69002 Lyons
Tel 78 37 40 11

Aix-en-Provence

4 Rue Joseph Cabassol
13100 Aix-en-Provence
Tel 23 31 92

Geneva

2/4 Rue de la Tour-de-Boel
1204 Geneva
Tel 28 33 40

Munich

Sendlingerstrasse
Munich West Germany
Tel 089 260 82 24

Hamburg

Neuer Wall 73-75
Hamburg West Germany

Brussels

81/83 Rue de Namur
Brussels Belgium
Tel 512 86 39

Maastricht

M. Smedenstraat 0
Maastricht Holland
Tel 043 509 72

The Hague

Papestraat 17
The Hague Holland
Tel 070 600540

Amsterdam

Singel 439/441
Amsterdam Holland
Tel 020 228087

AMERICAN SHOPS

San Francisco

735 Montgomery Street
San Francisco California
Tel 415 986 2325

1827 Union Street
San Francisco California
Tel 415 922 7200

New York

660 Madison Avenue
New York 10021

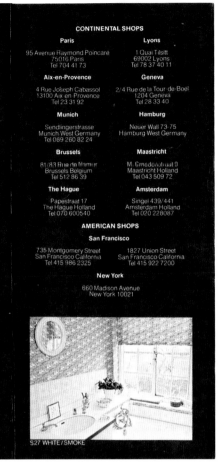

S27 WHITE/SMOKE

S56
Dk. Green/White
Emerald/White
Navy/White
White/Navy ■
Plum/Cream
Cream/Plum

Dk. Brown/White
White/Dk. Green
Smoke/Cream
Cream/Smoke
Terracotta/Cream
Cream/Terracotta ■

White/Dk. Brown ■

S65
White/Dk. Green
Saddle/Sand
Dk. Green/White
Dk. Brown/White ●
White/Dk. Brown ■
Plum/Cream

White/Navy
Cream/Plum
Smoke/Cream
Cream/Smoke
White/Scarlet ■
White/Moss

Navy/White
Scarlet/White ●
Moss/White

S57
White/Scarlet
White/Navy
White/Dk. Brown
Cream/Plum
Cream/Smoke
White/Moss

Cream/Thames
Sand/Saddle
White/Pink
Silver/Dk. Grey

■ **C.F.C. ONLY**

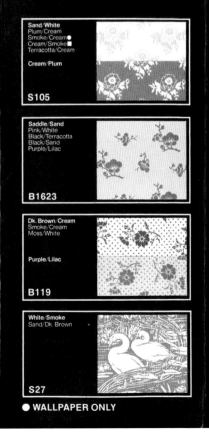

S105
Sand/White
Plum/Cream
Smoke/Cream ●
Cream/Smoke ■
Terracotta/Cream

Cream/Plum

B1623
Saddle/Sand
Pink/White
Black/Terracotta
Black/Sand
Purple/Lilac

B119
Dk. Brown/Cream
Smoke/Cream
Moss/White

Purple/Lilac

S27
White/Smoke
Sand/Dk. Brown

● **WALLPAPER ONLY**

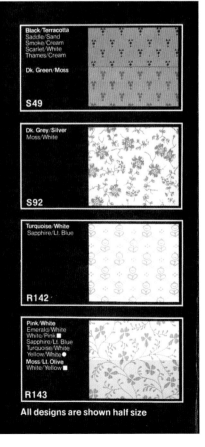

S49
Black/Terracotta
Saddle/Sand
Smoke/Cream
Scarlet/White
Thames/Cream

Dk. Green/Moss

S92
Dk. Grey/Silver
Moss/White

R142
Turquoise/White
Sapphire/Lt. Blue

R143
Pink/White
Emerald/White
White/Pink ■
Sapphire/Lt. Blue
Turquoise/White
Yellow/White ●
Moss/Lt. Olive
White/Yellow ■

All designs are shown half size

Laura Ashley Home Furnishings 1981

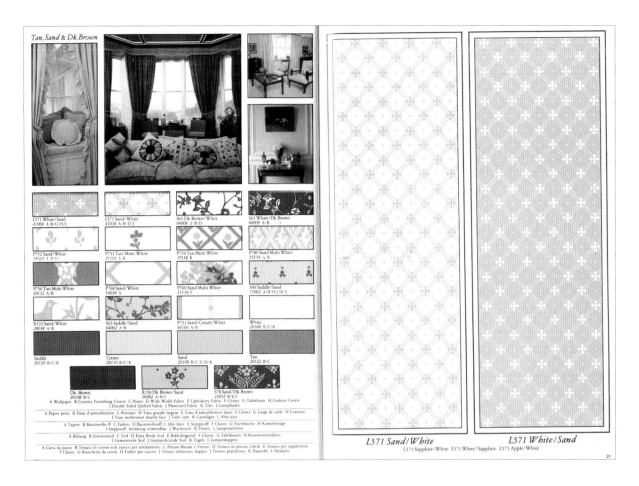

Tan, Sand & Dk.Brown

L571 White/Sand 41068 A/B/G/H/L	L571 Sand/White 41038 A/B/D/J	S65 Dk.Brown/White 04008 A/B/D	S65 White/Dk.Brown 04009 A/B
P752 Sand/White 33079 A/B/D	P753 Tan/Moss/White 16110 A/B	P754 Tan Multi White 17114 B	P789 Sand Multi White 13133 A/B
P756 Tan Multi White 49152 A/B	P768 Sand/White 54038 A	P769 Sand Multi White 55139 F	S49 Saddle/Sand 13002 A/B/H/J/K/L
R193 Sand/White 28038 A/B	S65 Saddle/Sand 04002 A/B	P751 Sand/Cream/White 44166 A/B	White 20100 B/C/K
Saddle 20120 B/C/K	Cream 20110 B/C/K	Sand 20109 B/C/E/H/K	Tan 20122 B/C
Dk.Brown 20108 B/C	R150 Dk.Brown/Sand 26062 A/B/I	S78 Sand/Dk.Brown 23052 B/E/I	

A.Wallpaper B.Country Furnishing Cotton C.Paints D.Wide Width Fabric E.Upholstery Fabric F.Chintz G.Tablelinen H.Cushion Covers I.Double Sided Quilted Fabric J.Plasticised Fabric K.Tiles L.Lampshades

A.Papier peint B.Tissu d'ameublement C.Peinture D.Tissu grande largeur E.Tissu d'ameublement épais F.Chintz G.Linge de table H.Coussins I.Tissu molletonné double face J.Toile ciré K.Carrelages L.Abat-jour

A.Tapete B.Baumwollstoff C.Farben D.Baumwollstoff 2·28m breit E.Steppstoff F.Chintz G.Tischwäsche H.Kissenbezüge I.Steppstoff, beidseitig verwendbar J.Wachstuch K.Fliesen L.Lampenschirme

A.Behang B.Interieurstof C.Verf D.Extra Brede Stof E.Bekledingsstof F.Chintz G.Tafellinnen H.Kussenovertrekken I.Gewatteerde Stof J.Geplastificeerde Stof K.Tegels L.Lampenkappen

A.Carta da parati B.Tessuto di cotone stile rustico per arredamento C.Pittura Murale e Vernici D.Tessuto in altezza 230cm E.Tessuto per tappezzeria F.Chintz G.Biancheria da tavola H.Fodere per cuscini I.Tessuto trafuntato doppio J.Tessuto plastificato K.Piastrelle L.Paralumi

L571 Sand/White   **L571 White/Sand**

L571 Sapphire/White   L571 White/Sapphire   L571 Apple/White

Poppy & Mustard

L577 Multi Poppy 42094 A/B	T215 Poppy/White 37083 A/B/H
P784 Poppy Multi White 57743 A/B	S49 Poppy/White 13083 A/B
P756 Tan Multi White 49152 A/B	L651 Mustard/Moss/White 56172 A/B/K
P754 Mustard Multi White 47148 B	P767 Poppy/Apple/White 33169 A/B/D/I
P784 Mustard Multi White 57148 A/B	L539 Red Multi White 43089 A/B/G/J/L
Mustard 20118 B/C/K	L651 Poppy/Apple/White 56169 A/B/I
P788 Mustard/White 38005 A/B	Poppy 20113 B/C

P752 White/Mustard 43001 A/B/E/H/J

A.Wallpaper B.Country Furnishing Cotton C.Paints D.Wide Width Fabric E.Upholstery Fabric F.Chintz G.Tablelinen H.Cushion Covers I.Double Sided Quilted Fabric J.Plasticised Fabric K.Tiles L.Lampshades

A.Papier peint B.Tissu d'ameublement C.Peinture D.Tissu grande largeur E.Tissu d'ameublement épais F.Chintz G.Linge de table H.Coussins I.Tissu molletonné double face J.Toile ciré K.Carrelages L.Abat-jour

A.Tapete B.Baumwollstoff C.Farben D.Baumwollstoff 2·28m breit E.Steppstoff F.Chintz G.Tischwäsche H.Kissenbezüge I.Steppstoff, beidseitig verwendbar J.Wachstuch K.Fliesen L.Lampenschirme

A.Behang B.Interieurstof C.Verf D.Extra Brede Stof E.Bekledingsstof F.Chintz G.Tafellinnen H.Kussenovertrekken I.Gewatteerde Stof J.Geplastificeerde Stof K.Tegels L.Lampenkappen

A.Carta da parati B.Tessuto di cotone stile rustico per arredamento C.Pittura Murale e Vernici D.Tessuto in altezza 230cm E.Tessuto per tappezzeria F.Chintz G.Biancheria da tavola H.Fodere per cuscini I.Tessuto trafuntato doppio J.Tessuto plastificato K.Piastrelle L.Paralumi

P784 Poppy Multi White

P784 Mustard Multi White   P784 Sapphire Multi White

company had seven shops in the United States and four in Canada with a further four shops, including Lenox Square in Atlanta, Georgia, due to open in 1980. It again proved to be a successful marketing tool.

Having dipped a toe in the water and found the idea to be a good one, they became more ambitious. The first proper catalogue was produced in 1981 and was a major expansion of the *Home Furnishings Room Planner*. It was seventy-two pages long and in four languages – English, French, German and Dutch. It sold for 50 pence a copy and had a print run of 50,000 copies. In the introduction the guiding aim was clearly stated: 'Natural fibres and wallpapers are the foundations of the collection. This has been expanded to 154 country furnishing cotton designs and colourways and 119 wallpapers for 1981.' At the time they had twenty-six shops in the United Kingdom and fifteen overseas, five of which were in Paris.[19]

The catalogue was a new departure on many fronts. They had begun to create room sets in the late 1970s for publicity photographs. At first they used the Ashleys' own houses, but after having decorated every room twice over they began to spread the net further afield using the houses of friends and sometimes customers. Sasha de Stroumillo and Tottie Whately both designed very original room sets for shop displays and for the catalogues. Sasha was at the time a punk – Bernard was forever threatening to cut off her hair spikes as a joke – but she had a wonderful grasp of the 'English romantic' look and instinctively knew how the company's image needed to be portrayed. The room sets to be photographed would be worked out as a pencil sketch and then the craftsmen set to work. Gradually the marketing team wanted to have their say, and as the co-ordinated look got a little out of hand Sasha had to remind them that there was such a thing as subtlety. Part of the brief was that the houses used as sets should always look lived in – the bed might be unmade, papers thrown on the floor in the sitting room, that sort of thing – partly because it brought life to what were staged and contrived photographs which could

ABOVE: A sketch for a room set for the 1987 catalogue. A very rare survivor, this was how the company stylist worked on producing the publicity material.

RIGHT: The room set created and photographed.

TOP LEFT: Catalogue for the 'Chintz Collection', which was first launched in 1981.

BOTTOM LEFT: An advert for the 'Decorator Collection', launched in 1982.

all too easily have been sterile. It made the photograph in the catalogue interesting and sometimes fun (there was one photograph of a mouse eating a piece of cake by a skirted table), but this was at times lost on marketing who objected to crumpled bedspreads.

The 1981 catalogue launched the 'Chintz Collection', while the 1982 edition launched the 'Decorator Collection', which was in fact never a huge success, in the United Kingdom at least. It was more popular in the United States. Laura had had lunch with the decorator John Fowler (who died in 1977) and it was after this meeting – probably arranged through Nancy Lancaster or Tom Parr who was then chairman of Colefax and Fowler – that the idea of a collection aimed at decorators was born.[20] It was a vehicle for some of Laura's more radical ideas that could be sold at a premium price without interfering with the general public's image of the brand.[21] Over the years Laura had found many interesting patterns which would not really have worked in the core retail collection. While they might not have appealed to her usual customers, she felt that they would be of interest to interior decorators and slightly more affluent customers. The 'Decorator Collection' started out in the decorator showroom, based in the Clapham Design Centre, but when the bargain shop at 71 Lower Sloane Street in London was refurbished in 1982, half the space was allocated to the collection, and the following year it took over the whole shop. Initially Laura assembled a small range, which was tested at an interior design exhibition held at the Barbican Centre in 1981. One of the staff involved recalled: 'Having exposed the new collection to the trade (professional decorators) we managed to get an idea of the direction in which we needed to go. The trade seemed to prefer multi-coloured prints and unusual, more sombre colours. Brights, such as sapphire and mustard couldn't possibly work in the context, and simply did not seem appropriate.'[22]

Gradually the collection evolved and it was decided to introduce two collections a year, both of which were to

be bold and innovative in design terms. The collection as a whole was radically different from the retail collection, but they were not unrelated. The 'Decorator Collection' shop at Lower Sloane Street in London was unlike any other Laura Ashley shop. It was designed as room sets with comfortable sofas and armchairs. Fabric was displayed in hanging lengths, with wallpapers displayed on flat boards and there was also a range of trimmings.

By 1982 the main retail range of prints had expanded to forty-three, of which twenty were two-tone and the remaining twenty-three multi-coloured. In 1983, using heavyweight cotton satin they launched the 'Drawing Room Fabric Collection', comprising seventeen new master prints. Most were large-scale patterns and, Laura explained, were 'wonderfully handsome, large prints which everyone is going to say are not like Laura Ashley at all but do in fact blend beautifully with all the small textured geometrics and small flowers which are our tradition.'[23] These collections were an attempt by Laura to change the public's taste. One of the staff recalled: 'Towards the end, Laura became quite frustrated at the way her customers would not keep up with her ideas; they lagged behind in a way she found infuriating.'[24]

In 1983 the company finally decided to name their prints. Hitherto they had used a letter and number code, the letter said to reflect the car registration letter for that particular year.[25] However, naming the prints became essential for marketing purposes because of the increase in press coverage both in newspapers and the ever-expanding number of style magazines. Describing a fabric as L539 was not quite as romantic or poetic as describing it as 'Wild Strawberry'. Curiously a magazine article in *House Beautiful* in August 1976 did contain many prints all of which were named, but as the magazine was published in the United States it may have been necessary to use names rather than codes in that market and it may well have been the initiative of their US marketing partner.

The interest in interior design and the continued growth of the home furnishings division led to the idea of producing a book to reflect what the Laura Ashley style was all about. Elizabeth Dickson was a freelance journalist covering style and fashion topics for many magazines and newspapers, having previously been London editor for *Architectural Digest*. Her association with the Ashleys went back to 1960 when, working on the *Evening Standard* newspaper, she wrote a small piece about the tea towels they were then producing.[26] The Laura Ashley company was always very helpful to journalists, freely supplying photographic transparencies for articles, which was not common practice. To any journalist, usually running to a tight deadline, the Ashleys were a godsend. Liz explained: 'You could ring up and ask if they had anything with roses, or something yellow, or whatever you wanted, and almost miraculously a transparency would arrive with just what you needed to finish a particular page.'[27] Of course it was, after all, a very cheap and effective way of getting the company exposure in the press, but it was a very rare attitude to take at the time. The numerous cuttings in the press books in the company's archive show the success of this simple and effective policy. It also engendered a huge amount of goodwill towards the company and meant that their product would usually be favourably received.

Liz was initially approached by Moira Braybrooke, the head of public relations, and asked if she would do a book for them. The project seemed to languish for a time, but was revived in 1981. Liz went to see an editor at Octopus Press armed with a basket of her cuttings, which the editor scarcely bothered to look through, and a deal was struck. It was likely the publisher who decided that the book should be a mixture of 'style' and 'how to'. *The Laura Ashley Book of Home Decorating* was largely created by Liz with Margaret Colvin doing the 'how to' section. Liz recalled: 'A friend lent me a studio for six weeks and a taxi turned up with a rather battered old suitcase full of trannies [photographic transparencies].' Liz set to work and created a flat plan,

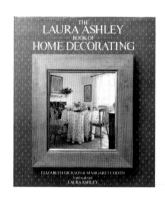

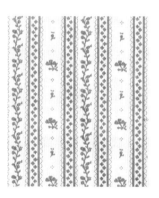

TOP: *The Laura Ashley Book of Home Decorating* published in 1983 was hugely successful and spawned a host of similar books.

BOTTOM: 'Meadowsweet' pattern L641, in lavender and sage green.

RIGHT: The principal guest bedroom at the British Embassy in Washington D.C. decorated in Laura Ashley products.

The guest sitting room
at the Embassy was also
decorated in company
products. The cotton satin
used for the curtains and
on the sofa is 'Victoria' from
the 'Decorator Collection'.

selecting and placing all the illustrations, and then wrote the text to fit the available space. She met Bernard and Laura, both in Wales and in France, flown over in the company plane, 'decked out in mauve or maroon *toile de Jouy*'. At one meeting at the chateau Nick and his wife, Ari, were so bored that they used the agenda to make paper darts – 'rather smart ones at that' – which they proceeded to fly out of the windows. It was a rather laissez-faire approach that was to characterize the whole project. Liz and Laura had supper together once at the Hyde Park Hotel and Liz found Laura 'both motherly and yet distant': supper finished rather early at 9 p.m. It seems surprising that the book was in fact created with very little input from Laura and Bernard. However, Liz was a very experienced journalist in whom they had every confidence. Using the material provided she produced a very evocative book in a mere six weeks, which she said 'reflects what I manipulated'.[28] Her manipulations captured the essence of the Laura Ashley style, showing how it could be used and how many of the effects could be achieved. It was an instant best-seller, with a revised edition published two years later and ultimately selling over 60,000 copies. At the time (1982/3) it was an innovative book with the clever mix of 'style' and 'how to' very unusual. The success of the book prompted a number of other books, many of which appeared after Laura died.

The Laura Ashley style really exploded in popularity in the 1970s. When Sir Nicholas Henderson was appointed British Ambassador in Washington D.C. and Lady Henderson discovered the state of the residence, it was hardly surprising that she turned to Laura for some help. In the diplomatic pecking order Paris and Washington are considered the plum posts. The Paris residence is a fine eighteenth-century *hôtel*, bought by the Duke of Wellington from Napoleon's sister, while the residence in Washington is far more recent. Designed by Sir Edwin Lutyens in 1929 it is one of only two Lutyens houses to be graced by a portico.[29] Lady Henderson was rather hampered by the reluctance of the Foreign and Commonwealth Office to allocate any funds for the residence, but she came up with the smart and practical idea of making the residence a showcase for British products and skills.

Lady Henderson invited a number of leading decorators to undertake the decoration of a room – David Mlinaric, John Stefanidis, David Hicks, Jean Munro and John Byrom were all involved – as was Laura who did the principle guest suite. The walls were papered in a blue and white stripe paper, with the curtains in a small print (a white pattern on a blue ground), the edge trimmed with the stripe taken from the wallpaper. The same small pattern was used for the upholstery; again the pattern was used both in the positive and the negative. One was used for the trim, while its opposite was the base pattern. Highlights were made by using the opposite combination for the cushions. The whole scheme, augmented with some decent furniture from the government collection, evoked the feeling of an English country house. Comfortable, elegant, but not really grand – perhaps 'homely' is a better description – it reflected what one would have expected to find in any number of country houses. The whole redecoration project was a great success, and Lady Henderson was able to pass on the residence in a far better state than she had found it. She and Laura also cemented a lifelong friendship.

The home furnishing fabrics were always closer to Laura's heart than the fashion side of the business, but it was to be the furnishing fabrics which, after Laura's time, partly dragged the company down. Bernard noted that in those days they might 'bring out say ten designs, only one of which would sell. So you held huge stocks' of fabric which didn't sell. 'Eventually this is what sank the company.'[30]

The Ashleys (with a small family friend) outside East Cottage in Limpsfield Chart in spring 1957. They lived in the cottage for five years. It was here that Laura's design philosophy was born.

HEARTH AND HOME

When they were first married, Laura and Bernard Ashley lived in rooms in Cheam in Surrey, which they rented for £4 a week. They then moved to Drayton Gardens in Chelsea, house-sitting for an elderly lady whilst she visited her son in Australia for six months. After this they set up home in an unfurnished flat at 56 St George's Square, Pimlico, at first on the ground floor and subsequently on the fifth floor. The flat was sparsely furnished, with just a few pieces of furniture, and bare floorboards, with baby Jane usually found crawling around covered in various colours of dye.[1] Here they remained until early 1955 (probably May), when Laura saw an advertisement for a cottage to rent on the Trevereux Manor estate near Limpsfield Chart in Surrey. The rent was a modest £1 10s. a week, which was a saving on the £2 5s. they were paying in Pimlico. By now they had two children – Jane and David: Nick was born in 1957 and Emma in Wales in 1965 – and the idea was that its rural location would give the family a better quality of life and, with its close proximity to London, it would be possible for Bernard to commute to Pimlico, where he maintained a print studio in Cambridge Street. Unfortunately the Suez crisis the following year resulted in petrol shortages, which prevented Bernard from commuting and severely hampered his ability to travel around the kingdom selling their products, necessitating a radical reappraisal of their plans.

East Cottage was small: it had a living room, scullery and a bedroom and bathroom on the ground floor, and two bedrooms above. The brick cottage with its oak beams and diamond mullions was set in the 'soft romantic Surrey countryside'. It had a profound effect on Laura: as Bernard recalled, it 'was as much a birthplace for Laura's philosophy on design and living as my Pimlico basement was for my ideas on machines. Although her childhood was largely spent walking over the mountains behind Merthyr Tydfil … it was the … hedgerows and small fields of rural Surrey that began to shape her ideas more fully.'[2] What Laura found in Limpsfield Chart were the dying embers of old English country life. The village was still a working, living village with many of the cottages still lived in by farm labourers and the like, not used as weekend bolt holes for the middle classes which is now so often the case. It was a completely different way of life from what she had know in Merthyr Tydfil (largely nineteenth-century industrial) or Wallington (thirties suburbia), more a hangover from the late nineteenth and eighteenth centuries, as chronicled by Gertrude Jekyll in *Old West Surrey* published in 1904 and in *Old English Household Life* published in 1925. Although a townie by birth, Laura was a countrywoman at heart and East Cottage suited her nature perfectly. It had a reasonably large garden and an orchard, so they were able to grow most of their own vegetables and they had an abundance of fruit. In the surrounding woods they gathered their own firewood – as cottagers had done for centuries – while in the orchard grazed goats that Laura would milk at 6 o'clock in the morning. Ever resourceful, she taught herself animal husbandry and kitchen gardening from books borrowed from the local public library.

After five idyllic years the lease of East Cottage was due to expire, and the estate did not wish to renew it, so Laura and Bernard began house hunting. In addition to difficulties in obtaining a mortgage, one of their main problems was that Bernard found it impossible to obtain any industrial development grants, which might have enabled him to build a textile printing factory in the immediate area, and he found the attitude of the local council officials – or 'goons',

as Bernard was apt to refer to all forms of officialdom – unhelpful. They decided to look for a new home elsewhere and Wales seemed an obvious place.

Laura packed her Mini and set off with the three children to Wales. They stayed at a campsite near Dolgellau and she sent Bernard a telegram saying where they were. The children found camping fun, but after six weeks, as the weather began to deteriorate, Laura found a static caravan on a site in Corris, not far from Machynlleth.[3] Using their modest savings and a small bank loan, Laura bought three small cottages in Maengwyn Street, Machynlleth, for the princely sum of £1,500. One of the cottages had a sitting tenant, but the other two provided living accommodation and a small shop of about 600 square feet. Eventually Bernard received another telegram simply saying: 'Shops open'.[4]

Machynlleth is a relatively small town and might not have appeared promising territory for them – the population was then a mere 2,000 – but the River Dovey (Dyfi) was famous for its salmon fishing, so the town had always had a healthy tourist trade. Gwalia House, as the three properties were known, was not large. Formerly a tailor's, it was a collection of six small rooms. There were four bedrooms on the second floor, a sitting room over the shop and a breakfast room over the adjoining cottage, all of which were served by two winding old oak staircases. The shop had blackened oak beams and a floor of Welsh slate; there was a grate on one side, with the staircase rising on the other. Bernard remarked, 'This was our first attempt at true interior design: we matched the traditional wooden beams and floors with old Welsh oak furniture, and the kitchen had its Welsh dresser, and a black-leaded oven which Laura loved to polish, just as she had been taught to do as a child in South Wales.'[5]

Perhaps what made the arrangement unusual was that Laura's kitchen in the second cottage opened into the shop, where they sold their own products such as neck scarves, tablemats, napkins and the like, but also local goods such as honey and even walking sticks. Laura was a great cook,

always baking or making jam, and the shop was permanently scented with the smell of freshly baked bread. Often Laura would be sewing or perhaps cutting something out on the kitchen table, which would all be cleared away for mealtimes.[6] The Ashleys were always hospitable people, even when they had very little to share, and gradually customers began to be offered a cup of coffee or tea and were even asked on impulse to lunch. Eventually Laura would specially prepare dishes for Saturday lunch, when she might easily entertain thirty guests. It was all very relaxed and friendly, and such open-hearted generosity earned the Ashleys great affection in the area.

In 1956 Bernard had moved his printing studio from Pimlico to Brasted in Kent, a mere four miles from home. He had rented an old coach house with 1,200 square feet of space, which gave ample room for his machine and for expansion. After the factory moved to Carno, some fifteen miles from Machynlleth, the Ashleys decided to look for a new home slightly nearer by. Perhaps they first saw Clogau on a bright sunny day in August, when its romantic setting swept aside more mundane considerations. Five miles from Carno and two from the nearest village of Pontdolgoch, the small eighteenth-century farmhouse was 1,500 feet up, and to make it accessible Bernard had to construct 'almost a mile of road'. Needless to say they were stranded by the first snow in the winter: it was, as a family friend recalled, 'one of BA's

impractical enthusiasms'.[7] A large old ash and a few larches sheltered the house, and with breathtaking views of the Welsh mountains it seemed to be on the very roof of the world and its appeal is obvious. In later years Laura wistfully remarked that the house they lived in subsequently, Rhydoldog, settled comfortably under a hill, had 'total peace rather than the eternal scream of the wind, which I somehow miss'.[8]

Clogau was a modest and simple house. When they bought it the house did need considerable work. It was made habitable and then Bernard knocked a way through into the old barn, incorporating it into the house to give a large sitting room some thirty feet by eighteen.[9] In the old house a partition wall was stripped of its lathes and plaster to reveal the old oak struts, helping to form a large kitchen-dining room. The floor was made of four black and four white tiles (probably lino), laid in a chequerboard pattern, upon which stood a large cherrywood circular table, light in colour, which toned well with pine. In the huge sitting room, down two broad steps, the room was dominated by a large rocking horse and three Welsh oak chests, six feet high with little brass handles, with 'top and bottom cupboards divided by drawers, all put to good use for clothes and linen storage'.[10] Simple whitewashed walls and a slate floor strewn with rugs completed the scene. In contrast the upholstered furniture was of a very modern kind, popular in the mid-1960s, and in rather striking and vivid colours. Bernard also built on a large flat-roofed extension at the rear, running the whole length of the property. This gave additional space in the kitchen as well as four bedrooms and a bathroom. Laura and Bernard's bedroom was up the narrow staircase in the old house, the bed resplendent with an old red and white quilt.

The whole family loved the house, especially the remote romantic setting surrounded by the hills and small mountain lakes where each year Arctic terns would come to breed. But for all that, it was hopelessly impractical in the winter, and on many occasions Bernard skied to work. In 1973 they began looking for a more convenient house with more space. The

children fought tooth and nail against any move, but that small insurrection was soon quelled. Eventually Bernard heard of the ideal house near Rhayader. They bought it, together with its estate of about a thousand acres.

Rhydoldog, as the house was known (it means 'water running over stones', an allusion to the nearby mountain stream), was a large house with some thirty rooms. Bernard recalled: 'Whenever we bought a house we had a fight – it lasted twenty-four hours,' but it was here that he and Laura were able to explore their talents for interior decoration.[11] Laura wrote, 'My own attitude towards decorating an old house is to find out all one can about the history of the house and even, if possible, the original colours used. I have no prejudices about colour but prefer to stand in a room and feel what it is asking for.'[12]

Originally a small farmhouse built in the seventeenth century by Thomas Oliver, a merchant, banker and farmer, the house had been extended in the eighteenth century and again in the nineteenth when his descendant, Ann Oliver (who inherited the estate on the death of her uncle, David Oliver), married John Ramsay Sladen, a native of Kent. The Sladens were originally from Folkestone, where they had been boat builders and in the smuggling business. He must have brought a considerable fortune with him, and this money enabled them to enlarge and re-plan the house. It was altered and extended again in the late nineteenth century, when the Birmingham Corporation bought some of the estate to form the Elan reservoir, completed in 1898. To reconcile these various stages of development, the house was part stuccoed and the upper portion tile hung. It is not a beautiful house, but has a certain quirky charm and a presence. It is also in a magnificent position, and this was undoubtedly one of the main attractions for Laura and, particularly, Bernard, who retained a huge affection for the house.

When the Ashleys bought the house in 1973, it was in a good state of structural repair – the previous owner, having a passion for engineering, had updated the plumbing and the

electrical wiring – so the Ashleys merely had to redecorate. There was more scope here for imagination and interpretation than at Clogau: whereas Clogau was small, simple and rustic, Rhydoldog was far grander and more complex, being a mixture of 'old Welsh farmhouse, Georgian and finally and probably dominantly, Victorian Gothic'. With such a muddle the 'only answer was to decorate each room exactly to its own period and this we did'.[13] At this time furnishing fabrics made up a very small proportion of the company's turnover, but by 1978 this had radically changed and they made up just under half the turnover. Undoubtedly good fortune played a part, but the decoration of Rhydoldog helped to crystallize the Laura Ashley home image, for here the Ashleys had a canvas upon which to experiment.

Initially the house was decorated in quite a different style. It was featured in *House Beautiful* in August 1976 with the original decoration, which was heavily influenced by contemporary taste. As the Ashleys' knowledge and understanding grew, and perhaps as their research developed into old patterns, the desire to be more faithful to the house grew, and they decided to do some redecoration.

Ringing the bell in the Gothic porch, visitors were ushered into a long L-shaped Victorian hall. Laura and her design team had discovered a small trellis pattern by the nineteenth-century architect, designer and writer, Owen Jones, which they adapted and printed in brown and greys to tone with the encaustic tiled floor. Halls can be tricky to decorate and quite easily end up resembling hotel corridors, but Laura sought to make theirs an ante-room to the rooms that opened off it – a clever and astute move. Faded oriental carpets, oak furniture and a large bookcase filled with suitable old tomes acted as a prelude to the library, opening off the hall to the north. This was Bernard's room and he chose all the furniture, which he allied with a plum colour scheme, partly because he found it restful but also because it gave the room warmth.

TOP: A family breakfast on the terrace at Rhydoldog.

MIDDLE: The conservatory at Rhydoldog, a combination of every Gothic conservatory Laura had seen.

BOTTOM: 'Lady Fern', used for both the wallpaper and curtaining of the drawing room.

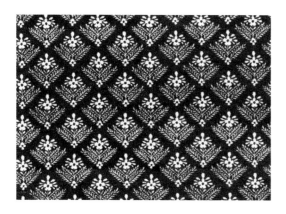

By far the grandest room in the house was the huge Gothic drawing room, and it was also the most uncompromisingly Victorian. At first, they decorated the room in a more contemporary manner. Using just one fabric – christened 'Glenartney' in *House Beautiful* (although later known as 'Lady Fern'), retailed as S78 – Laura papered the walls and used the same pattern and colourway for the curtains. Before the nineteenth-century pine mantel, in a rather delicate neo-Adam style, they set a large Chinese Aubusson rug in yellow and beige, upon which stood two quite modern-looking sofas in a deep russet brown. Scattered on the sofas were a collection of patchwork cushions, all created from the many small prints the company was then producing. The room was comfortable and very much a reflection of the era. Eventually, Laura and Bernard decided that the hideous windows needed to be altered and that the house cried out for a conservatory to take advantage of the glorious view down the Wye valley. Laura remarked: 'It seemed strange in fact that the house hadn't got a conservatory already and now that it has everyone imagines it has always been there it looks so right.'[14] In a way she was correct: the house did at one time have a conservatory, but it was to the side of the house rather than the face. Luckily the Ashleys readily obtained planning permission and they commissioned local builders to build what Laura described as 'a composite of all the Gothic-style conservatories I had ever seen'.[15]

Sometimes, as Laura had observed, rooms themselves decide what colours they are to be decorated and the drawing room wanted crimson. Laura longed for blue and gold, but crimson it was. A friend had a nineteenth-century chenille rug, by then almost in tatters, and Laura persuaded a carpet company to copy the pattern and make one in Brussels weave in crimson, with a putty-colour background. At the time Brussels-weave carpets were enjoying a renaissance, following their revival by the decorator John Fowler.[16] The wallpaper, picking up the carpet colours, looked like another Owen Jones pattern (which it might well be) but was in fact

The drawing room in the 1980s in its full Victorian glory. The wallpaper was a copy of a design (possibly by Owen Jones) found at Harewood House, Yorkshire, and the curtain fabric was copied from fragments found on the footboard of a bed at Clifton Castle. The carpet is a Brussels weave which was marketed through the 'Decorator Collection'.

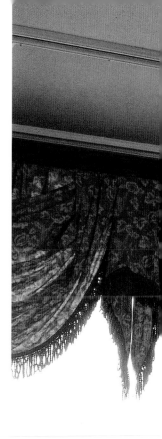

copied from an old design found at Harewood House in Yorkshire, which had been radically altered by Sir Charles Barry in the nineteenth century. Saying 'You have to be single minded when decorating' and one must be rather autocratic and pay no heed to 'sulking husbands and children', Laura scoured the salerooms and was able to acquire some very fine pieces of Victorian furniture, which at the time you couldn't give away.[17] She thus acquired a fine mahogany bookcase, a massive Gothic side table and a rather eclectic mixture of chairs and sofas. Allied to all this were a collection of prints (very much Bernard's domain), a couple of sets of antlers, and various feather and shell concoctions under glass domes. Victorian paraffin lamps, mercifully converted to electricity, and the odd bust of a poet set upon a large skirted table weighted down with bullion fringe, completed the high Victorian look.

Of course no Victorian drawing room would have been complete without swag and tail draperies, and these were copied from an old upholsterer's pattern book, probably Thomas King's *The Upholsterers' Accelerator*, published in 1833. When the drawing room was finished, Laura thought the result magnificent and 'distinctly like the interior of a hunting lodge in a Walter Scott novel'. The children thought it looked like the 'Lord Mayor of Manchester's parlour', and as (unbeknown to them) Manchester Town Hall is a masterpiece of high Victorian Gothic by Alfred Waterhouse, they were probably not far off the mark.[18]

Beyond a Gothic arch in the hall the corridor opened into the staircase hall in the Georgian part of the house. The beautiful oak staircase flowed down into this hall, terminating in an elegant swirl. Thus the mood changed from the Gothic to the classical, and rather than use the Owen Jones geometric wallpaper, the Ashleys used a Regency stripe in apricot and a soft aquamarine – a subtle change in colour as well as pattern. This colour scheme was picked up in the print room, which served as Laura's sitting room and her office. Here she used apricot moiré wallpaper, edged by a grisaille border.

TOP: The elegant swirl of the eighteenth-century banister.

BOTTOM: The print room, Laura's sitting room and her office.

RIGHT: The print room. The pendant curtain pelmet was copied from the Chinese drawing room at the Royal Pavilion, Brighton.

The prints themselves were taken from eighteenth-century books and printed up at the factory, as were the garlands and bows, all of which were then meticulously cut out by ladies at the factory and mounted on gauze, so that they could be removed if the need arose. Laura also used apricot moiré to make the curtain pelmet, which was in the form of pendants, copied from a design for the Chinese drawing room at the Royal Pavilion, Brighton. The curtains were a simple pale stripe in apricot and aquamarine, carrying on the colours in the hall.

Like the print room, the dining room was in the eighteenth-century part of the house. When they first decorated the room it had quite a modern feel, even if the tables were nineteenth-century. The chairs were certainly modern, with rush seats and a severe design, all because 'the men are rather heavy around here and I was afraid antique chairs would be dangerous for them', and presumably the men dangerous for the chairs.[19] The walls seem to have been a plain cream, but Laura used 'Monan's Rill' for the curtains. Described as a 'fantasy of trees, flowers, birds and beasts that never were', it was in a heather mauve, and Laura repeated the fabric for the welted tablecloth. Napkins were in the same pattern, only different colourways, and the table usually had an overcloth in a tiny sprigged flowered pattern called 'Guinevere'.

The dining room had been altered by the addition of a late Victorian or Edwardian bay window, so Laura made the room into an Edwardian room. At Wythenshawe Hall in Manchester she and Bernard found a fragment of eighteenth-century flock wallpaper, and the large scale of the pattern masked the ambiguities of the room. As an experiment it was printed up in brown on a nutmeg ground, but was never actually put into production. Laura pointed out, 'in candle light with a brightly burning fire it is stunning, and in summer it looks cool and makes a frame for the wonderful views'.[20] This would indeed have been the case, for the yellow glow from candlelight or fire would have enhanced the colour

scheme beautifully. Edwardian draperies and curtains in the same pattern completed the effect. The room was filled with dining room chairs and a table in the Queen Anne revival style, which were Laura's mother's, and these lived happily beside a Liberty cabinet, a good solid piece of Arts and Crafts furniture. A collection of blue and white china filled an alcove, and the walls were adorned with a small collection of Welsh landscape pictures in gilt frames. The effect was not grand, far less pretentious; the room had a comfortable middle-class, even bourgeois air to it.

The kitchen lay beyond a baize door in the oldest part of the house. It was very much a farmhouse kitchen, with a well-scrubbed table, pine dresser and a Rayburn cooker. The terracotta tiles were strewn with rugs and it was here at the Rayburn that Laura liked to think. It was also where she would often hold her design meetings, the staff being served apple crumble and custard, as if she believed that robust country food helped to comfort the mind and ease thoughts.

Rhydoldog was a family house, but it was also the company 'hotel'. As the business grew and expanded, managers and key staff from far-flung outposts would come to the factory and many stayed at the house. Perhaps some found staying with the boss intimidating but the hospitality the Ashleys offered at home was part of the family atmosphere that was the hallmark of the business. A favourite room with guests was the room immediately at the top of the staircase. Once grey, it was so no longer, for Laura did it in pink and a mossy green. The wallpaper was an old Victorian pattern, a small flower stripe in pink on an off-white ground. The curtains were a candy stripe bound on the edge in moss green.

The master bedroom over the drawing room was a large room that was decorated twice: once to Bernard's design and once to Laura's. Bernard chose the first scheme and he produced a rather masculine composition in plum and cream. At the time (the early 1970s) the company was beginning to produce small-scale positive-negative patterns that seem now, in retrospect, to exemplify the period. The curtains, bed hangings and quilt were all in a plum version of 'Wild Clematis', which was teamed with cream trellis wallpaper. It might seem that these two relatively small-scale prints would have been rather busy together, but they complemented one another, as their pattern bases were quite different.[21] Most of the furniture Bernard chose was masculine too, and it all worked well together. When Laura redecorated the room a few years later, the room took on a more feminine air, perhaps reflecting how tastes were developing and changing in the 1970s. She copied a Victorian rose print design from a nineteenth-century pelmet, and used this for curtains, quilt and half-tester bed canopy, a very Victorian creation. This was lined with a small rosebud design, which was also used to upholster a sofa in the window. The walls were not papered but dragged in pink emulsion (pink over white) and edged by a swagged border. Pieces of painted and lacquered furniture together with an Aubusson rug completed the effect.

Opening off the master bedroom was Laura's dressing room. It was decorated to harmonize with the earlier plum bedroom scheme, so a small thistle sprig pattern in burgundy and moss green on a cream ground was used for the walls, the burgundy being picked up by the curtains and upholstery. To help anchor the pattern, the walls were edged with a border of burgundy berries and mossy green leaves, but in a larger scale than that on the walls. Laura's bathroom was done in a relaxed style, with a slipper chair or window seat on which to sit, perhaps to admire the numerous small prints with which the walls were adorned.

The Ashley children's rooms were all very individual. Jane, the eldest, chose a room in the seventeenth-century part of the house, partly because it reminded her of Clogau. Emma, the youngest, chose a room over the dining room in the Georgian part of the house. She was nine when they moved in and one of the things she asked for was a white painted floor. She got it, with a big rug in the middle. The four-poster bed was dressed in yellow, edged in green, and

LEFT: The master bedroom as originally decorated to Bernard's design: the curtains and bedspread are in 'Wild Clematis', a hugely popular print.

BELOW: Pattern G398 was used for the wallpaper in the Grey room, the principal guest bedroom.

ABOVE: 'Country Roses', the Victorian rose print fabric Laura used.

RIGHT: The master bedroom in its final form as decorated by Laura.

CLOCKWISE FROM TOP:

Emma's room in its first form with a white painted floor.

She arrived home from school to find the room redecorated.

David's room at the top of the house in deep blue.

The same room redecorated in numerous shades of white.

the window curtains were in an off-white. The furniture was mostly stripped pine, then all the rage. In 1983 she came home to find it had been transformed. The room was bedecked by an eighteenth-century design of sprigs of roses and ribbons. It was used on the walls, curtains, quilt and bed hangings, which were back lined with a small pink and white sprig design, the bed curtains being edged by a double frill, then a popular finish. Lacquer furniture replaced the pine to give a very romantic air.

David and Nick were billeted on the second floor. David's room was very bold. The walls were painted a heavy navy blue and the roof spars were picked out in brilliant white. He wanted an uncluttered look – 'nothing namby-pamby', as he put it – and to that end even the pillows were replaced by a bolster. Like Emma's room, David's was later redecorated, with the heavy blue (which must have been a nightmare to paint over) being replaced by different shades of white: a grey white near the window toning back into a creamy white further from the source of light. As the room was one of the largest in the house, it eventually gained a four-poster bed – the headboard made from an old church pew that Bernard had found – with bed curtains in a print inspired by an Elizabethan design of acorns and oak leaves, printed on a cream background.

Nick, the younger son, did the swag and tail thing. What became Nick's room had been intended to be Laura's design studio, but never worked as such. She much preferred the print room and the kitchen table. Nick remarked, 'For my first bedroom, I did a fairly traditional Laura Ashley look. But for this one, I wanted to react against the soft country look that they were doing in 1977.'[22] He used a deep royal blue, lighter in tone than the blue his brother's room had been, and he set this off with sparkling white paintwork. The bed canopy and curtains were done in a monochrome pattern in tones of cream and sandy yellow, and the bed hangings, bedspread and valance and window draperies were trimmed with yard upon yard of bullion fringe. One would have thought such

TOP: Jane's room was in the old part of the house. Here it is arranged for a catalogue shoot in the early 1980s.

BOTTOM: Nick's room in full 'swag and tail' mode.

127

TOP: The library at Remaisnil decorated in Bernard's masculine scheme.

BOTTOM: The staicase hall, simply decorated. The tablecloth is made from 'Venetia'.

a room cried out for carpet, or at least a huge rug, but Nick varnished the floorboards and left them bare, save for small runners by the bed and a slightly larger rug in the centre of the room.

Laura and Bernard lived at Rhydoldog for seven years, but the penal rates of taxation levied in the late 1970s were a huge worry for them. At the very last possible moment, in the first days of April 1977 they left Rhydoldog. 'The wild daffodils were smothering the banks of the old water garden and thousands more nodded to me all the way down the lovely driveway to say farewell,' Laura said.[23] They were never to return.

Leaving Rhydoldog was hard for both Laura and Bernard, but Laura especially missed her beloved Wales and felt the loss keenly. They settled in Brussels and in northern France, where they bought the Chateau de Remaisnil near Abbeville in 1979, between the towns of Arras and Amiens. Unlike Rhydoldog, Remaisnil was a consistent architectural composition, having been built around 1760. A central limestone bay flanked by projecting wings in brick with limestone dressings, which render the brick in the minority. A sale in 1909 had destroyed some original eighteenth-century interiors, so some alterations and restorations had been made around the time of the Great War. By the time the Ashleys bought the house it required complete renovation and restoration.

Remaisnil might appear vast, but in fact was merely one room deep. The central bay contained the saloon (or *grand salon*), flanked on either side by ante-rooms, which were in turn flanked by the library and staircase hall in the south wing, and the dining room and kitchen in the north wing. On the first floor the bedrooms opened off a long corridor – there was no corridor on the ground floor, as all the rooms interconnected – and on the second floor the single space was divided up to give a series of small bedrooms.

The purchase of Remaisnil coincided with a change in emphasis for the company: a gradual shift from the cottage

ABOVE LEFT: The *petit salon*, Laura's sitting room. The curtains are in 'Emmeline'.

LEFT: The *grand salon*.

RIGHT: The *grand salon*, with ornate curtains made by Hammonds and Co., was kept relatively formal.

style, which had hitherto been its hallmark, to a slightly grander, more country-house look. This change was probably a natural progression but could have been partly inspired by Remaisnil. It took two years to get the fabric of the building in order before any decoration could be undertaken.

The entrance to the house was through the south wing, the hall dominated by an oak cantilever staircase. A slightly unusual touch was the floor, laid in three shades of marble. The hall was sparsely furnished, with a rustic table and four country chairs. A large Brussels tapestry brought a splash of colour to the otherwise beige and white colour scheme, further enlivened by a deep red stair carpet. The library opened off to the right and stood aloof from the grand enfilade formed by the other reception rooms. It had probably once been the dining room (the plasterwork is very hunting, shooting, fishing in all its detail) and it lay in close proximity to the old kitchens, which were in a *commun* separate from the house, although joined in the nineteenth century by a tunnel. Such arrangements were by no means unusual at that time, as fire was a constant fear. The Ashleys chose to decorate the library in the English manner, with comfortable chairs and sofas. A colour scheme of green was chosen – both dark and pale to emphasize the *boiseries* or panelling. Cream moiré was used in panels and the same pattern was used for the festoon curtains. This was the most relaxed room and was used as an everyday sitting room.

In contrast, a pair of double doors at the bottom of the stairs led into the *petit salon*, the small saloon or ante-room, the first of the parade rooms. It was arranged as a drawing room, with swagged draperies over white poles, the swags trimmed in sage green and the tails similarly back lined. While these curtains were grand, the fabric used was distinctly modest; a simple cotton floral print in sand on a white ground, actually based on a *toile de Jouy* design. Originally the furniture was all eighteenth century and French, but that soon changed. Comfortable upholstered furniture brought an English informality, and the curtains too were altered.

OPPOSITE: The kitchen.

TOP: The dining room, with curtains in 'Nutmeg' and a tablecloth in 'Venetia'.

BOTTOM: The dining room, with new curtains in 'Blue Ribbons'.

133

LEFT: The breakfast room in red and white *toile de Jouy*.

ABOVE: The red and white *toile*, a favourite pattern of Laura's.

TOP: The bedroom corridor in blue and creamy white.

BOTTOM: The Ritz bedroom, named after the hotel in Paris.

OPPOSITE: The coral fabric in the Ritz room was copied from an eighteenth-century Lyons silk.

They retained the old swagged draperies but replaced the curtains with a floral print, 'Emmeline' F127, on a sand ground.

Walking through another set of doors you found yourself in the *grand salon*, which sat in the centre of the house as the principal reception room. It was more flamboyant than the restrained neo-classical elegance of the *petit salon*, probably dating from around the time the house was built. In keeping with tradition, the Ashleys kept the room relatively sparsely furnished, with a few chairs, a sofa, a harpsichord and four small consoles in the Louis XV style, which Laura had made. The six windows – three to either side – were dressed in rose pink silk, the colour reflecting the tones found in the eighteenth-century carpet. These were the most magnificent draperies Laura ever had made and were richly trimmed with bullion, a large gimp, rope and tassels.

Beyond the *grand salon* lay the small dining room or breakfast room, balancing the *petit salon* to the south. There was no fireplace in the room, merely a semi-circular niche that might once have held a fountain or a tiled stove. The panelling was contemporary with the *grand salon*, but without its Rococo exuberance. Laura found a *toile de Jouy* design of peacocks with sheep, beehives and a few figures set in a rural landscape. She printed it up in a bold raspberry red and – for this is the trick when using *toile* – used it for the curtains and the upholstery. It was everywhere: even the under-cloth under the tablecloth was made of *toile*.

The dining room lay in the north wing and was actually the billiard room when the Ashleys bought the house. Like the *petit salon*, it was a restrained essay in the neo-classical style. While the breakfast room was a wholly French affair, the dining room was more English in character with a Gillows extending table, which could comfortably seat two dozen, around which were gathered a set of Regency mahogany chairs. Like a number of other rooms, it was decorated and later modified to provide illustrations for the company's catalogues, usually to display a new fabric, which often meant new curtains. A small-scale print in cream and burgundy

LEFT: Laura's bedroom in pink and white.

TOP: Laura's bedroom. The scalloped edge to the pelmet was inspired by a drawing of Madame Jeoffrin's bedchamber in Paris, drawn by Hubert Robert in about 1770.

BOTTOM: Bernard's bedroom, a strongly masculine room. The bed, curtains and walls are covered in a small trellis pattern.

BELOW: The Empire bedroom, filled with their collection of Empire furniture. The window curtains and bed corona are of white muslin.

OPPOSITE: A modern view across the garden, largely created by Laura and Bernard.

was used in panels on the walls, and the same design was printed up for the curtains, which were cotton with swagged-and-tailed draperies in a Regency pattern, bedecked with a burgundy fringe, rosettes and cord-and-tassel tiebacks. The new kitchen created next door was designed by Laura to be a practical and functional room. The scrubbed pine worktops belied the fact that modern conveniences were hidden away, for all had to be pretty to behold as well as practical and convenient.

The red-carpeted staircase led up to the landing and the bedroom corridor in a cool colour scheme of smoky blue and white. Along the length of the corridor the windows, with elegant tailored pelmets and curtains, conveyed a sense of rhythm, and pieces of painted furniture provided punctuation. Each of the bedrooms that opened off it was decorated in a distinct style, all unmistakably French in character. The principal guest bedroom was known as the Ritz room, so named after the hotel in Paris. The rich coral coloured fabric was copied from an eighteenth-century Lyons silk, and Laura used it generously, for the draperies and curtains, the bedspread and over-valance, and also the bed festoons – practically hanging the room in it. She copied the festoons around the bed alcove from an eighteenth-century drawing depicting such an arrangement in a royal palace.

The chateau afforded more opportunities for historical research than their previous homes, and this research was on display in the Louis XVI room next door. The inspiration for dressing the *lit de polonaise* came from an eighteenth-century watercolour depicting such a bed, topped by plumes of feathers, but hung in the same fabric as the walls and curtains. Laura stopped short of going that far, instead using a striped wallpaper as a foil to another fabric copied from an eighteenth-century Lyons silk.

Laura's room was an altogether more restrained affair. A Sèvres porcelain plaque was the inspiration for the room's decoration. A bold pink and white striped silk was used for the curtains and to partly line the walls. The bed stood between a pair of concave cupboards, so it seemed logical to create slightly convex pelmet boards for both the curtains and the bed pelmet; the edge was also scalloped with a large and small partial radius. Bernard's room lay at the end of the corridor. Like all his rooms it was unmistakably masculine, done in shades of smoke blue and cream, deeper in tone and weight than the blue in the corridor. A small trellis design wallpaper was used to line the larger panels, and a matching fabric was used for the bed cover and the window curtains. Again the pattern is classic Laura Ashley. It continued in the adjoining bathroom, which, together with another small room that served as his private office, formed Bernard's own suite.

The Empire bedroom, above the dining room and looking out over the landscape, was the last of the string of bedrooms. A small collection of Empire furniture – hence the name of the room – was gathered together and set against aquamarine moiré wallpaper, with the architectural detailing of the walls picked out in white and grey. The bed was given an elegant corona, inspired by Robert Smirke's drawing of Madame Récamier's bedroom as it was in 1802.[24] White muslin edged by a white bullion fringe created a light effect, carried on by the window curtains, swags of muslin held aloft by a large choux. Unlike the bed draperies, the window curtains were not lined, creating a pale translucence.

Rhydoldog had little or no garden – with such a stunning setting a garden and flowers seemed unnecessary. It was at the chateau that Laura was able to indulge in her love of gardens and gardening, a particularly British passion. The chateau was set between two magnificent avenues of limes leading east and west; originally two further avenues would have led north and south. When the Ashleys bought the property, its once extensive estate had dwindled and the garden and park were little more than 25 acres. Immediately around the chateau were the remains of formal gardens – gravel paths, neat lawns and a few fine trees. On the south lawn stood a statue of Pan, and around the *commun* a series of steel arches carried an array of climbing roses, clematis and jasmine. In the sunken garden a neglected old conservatory was restored and turned into the greenhouse. The Ashleys replanted very much in the English manner, rather in the style of the walled garden at Haseley Court, belonging to Nancy Lancaster, whom they knew. Hornbeam hedges created avenues, and rose-festooned arches created doorways into a garden of old French roses, a garden of herbs, a vegetable garden and so forth. But in the early days the house took most of the available time and money as gradually the interior was put in order.

Clogau, Rhydoldog and Remaisnil were all houses in the country, some more remote than others, but Bernard and Laura also decorated a couple of town houses. As the business grew, they acquired a house at 23 Paultons Square, Chelsea, in 1970. While there seem to be no surviving photographs to give an exact idea of the decoration, in the early 1980s the company bought 23 Campden Street in Kensington, which was decorated as a showcase for the company's products, and the whole project was described in a book, *Laura Ashley Decorates a London House*, written by Jane Clifford and published by the company in 1985. Built in 1862, the four-storey brick and stucco house was quite typical of London. The Ashleys decorated the entrance hall in paper of an Owen Jones design, copied from a pattern book of wallpapers printed by Townsend, Parker & Co. in 1855.[25] Actually the hall was a trifle gloomy, but this was deliberate, following the advice of John Claudius Loudon and his *Encyclopaedia of Cottage, Farm and Village Architecture*, which was published in 1833 and ran to numerous editions.

The drawing room was another essay in high Victorian taste. Again an Owen Jones paper was used, drawn from the same pattern book and in tones of buff. The skirting boards were 'grained' to imitate mahogany, although at the end of the nineteenth century they probably would have been painted with white paint. The Ashleys used the same type of Brussels-weave carpet as that in the drawing room at Rhydoldog, edged by a broad border of acanthus leaves and

a Grecian key, the red being picked up by crimson sateen with a Tudor rose design that was found on a nineteenth-century settee. Although not a Pugin pattern, it has similarities to one of his patterns used at the Palace of Westminster and at Windsor Castle.

A small geometric pattern, similar to the wallpaper but on a much smaller scale, was used for the upholstery. For the most part the furniture was French, dating from the mid-nineteenth century. It was arranged following a drawing by Gillows of Lancaster and was typically Victorian. The morning room was lighter in tone and as the room lacked a cornice, or any architectural detail, they used a *trompe l'oeil* foliage border. The white lily and carnation chintz was copied from an early nineteenth-century design in the Whitworth Art Gallery in Manchester and made up following a design from Thomas King's *The Upholsterers' Accelerator*.

Kitchen and dining room were a compromise: the two basement rooms were knocked together and curtains used to conceal the kitchen when dining. A rope-edge border ran around the edges of the walls to give definition and help anchor the room, and was also used on the curtains and their attached valance. The chintz – 'Clandon Bell' – was again copied from the Whitworth Art Gallery. The chipboard dining table was covered with a cloth in 'Seaweed', a small foliage pattern that was also used to cover the seats of the dining chairs. This small-scale pattern worked with the chintz and the old oriental carpet.

While at Remaisnil, which was fine as a country retreat, the Ashleys realized that they really needed a city base. They both knew Brussels – Bernard's family had friends there and Laura had been based there during the war – so it seemed a natural choice. It was also convenient for a new factory at Helmond in the Netherlands. They found a grand town house on the rue Ducal, overlooking the Parc de Bruxelles. The house was in a deplorable state. It is reputed to have been the French Embassy at the time of the Battle of Waterloo. Gutted by fire just before the First World War, the house had been

CLOCKWISE FROM FAR LEFT:

The morning room in Campden Street had no architectural detail such as a cornice, so a printed border was added.

The pelmet was taken from a design by Thomas King from his famous 1848 book.

A nineteenth-century chintz design, copied from the Whitworth Art Gallery in Manchester and christened 'White Bowen'.

The simple dining room, created in the basement next to the kitchen.

'Clandon Bell', used for the dining room curtains.

'Seaweed' was used for the chair seats in the same room.

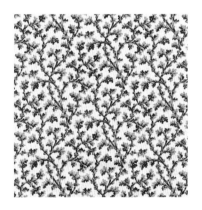

RIGHT: The drawing room in Campden Street, looking towards the bay windows. The room strongly recalls a drawing by Gillows of Lancaster which showed the arrangement of furniture in a similar room.

LEFT: The geometric wallpaper is an Owen Jones design taken from a pattern book produced by Townsend, Parker and Co. in 1855.

BELOW: The drawing room, looking away from the bay windows. The tudor rose design on the crimson sateen fabric used for the curtains could have been designed by Pugin.

restored, but after the Second World War had become offices, the elegant rooms chopped up and divided by partition walls. The Ashleys ripped all these out and gradually, as the breezeblocks were thrown in the skips, the elegance of the rooms was revealed. With the house having so chequered a history only Laura's bedroom supplied any information on the historical decoration; elsewhere Laura had only her own taste to guide her, and she decorated each room around a theme.

Passing through the archway from the street, entering the house on the left – to the right a few unconnected rooms were turned into company offices – led immediately to the staircase hall. A trellis pattern paper in cream and grey, picking up the fine black and white chequered marble floor, ran up the staircase. This unified the space and provided a foil to the eclectic mixture of furniture, objects and pictures. Overlooking the street was the dining room, which Laura decorated in the English style, with a double pillar dining table and Sheraton chairs. An English chintz covered the chair seats and was used for the curtains, while the walls were hung with green damask, picking up the colour from the curtains.

The staircase led up to the rotunda, a sort of ante-room to the suite of reception rooms that followed, occupying the first floor. Fortunately under the lino tiles the room still had its original parquet floor, which could be restored. The walls were marbled in shades of yellow, which provided a good contrast to the watercolour gallery beyond, and also to the *salon*. Running the width of the house, the *salon* was full of light. Laura had always wanted a yellow drawing room. The idea was probably influenced by Nancy Lancaster's yellow drawing room at Avery Row in Mayfair, but what Laura created in the *salon* was quite different. She used yellow for the panels and picked out the stiles and rails and details of the *boiseries* in French grey. To this she added lilac, used in the upholstery and in the carpet, and also a subtle lilac grey for a pair of glazed cabinets she designed and had made, their legs

LEFT: Laura's yellow, grey and lilac *salon* on the first floor with views over the Parc de Bruxelles. This was very much Laura's room and it fulfilled a wish for a yellow drawing room. The walls were papered in panels of yellow moiré in imitation of silk fabric. The curtains were in yellow silk moiré with *tête flamande* (Flemish heading), now known as goblet pleats.

ABOVE: Grey was used to set off the panels of yellow, and lilac tablecloths acted as accent notes in the scheme.

ABOVE: A corner of the library.

OPPOSITE: The library was arranged and furnished in the English style for the 1986 catalogue. The curtains are Linen Union in 'Grapes', while the throw over the Knole sofa is 'Florentina'.

echoing the legs of a set of Louis XVI chairs arranged around the room.

The other large room was the library. This was decorated more to Bernard's taste and was therefore more masculine in character than the adjacent *salon*. After the fire just before the Great War the panelling had been restored, although it would seem in a different style, for stylistically it was of a later date than all the other decoration. The initial idea had been to pick out the detailing with gilding, but it soon became obvious that the end result would be reminiscent of an over-decorated hotel dining room. As with so many things in decoration, it was a question of balance: an eighteenth-century gilded room can look magnificent, while exactly the same scheme executed last week can look hopelessly naff. So to avoid any such impression the Ashleys toned down their design. The furniture was an eclectic mixture, dominated by a Knole sofa in blue-grey, upon which were scattered numerous cushions worked by Laura.

The final room in this collection of reception rooms was a small corner room used as Bernard's study. As in the watercolour gallery, the Ashleys used grey moiré-effect wallpaper, and grey moiré for the curtains, which had goblet pleats and festoons of silver cord and tassels. It was very much a working room, with a large painted bookcase specifically designed for his many files and a large mahogany table strewn with all his papers.

Laura's bedroom overlooked the Parc de Bruxelles. Although the room had been divided, when the modern partition walls came down it became apparent that the bed had once stood in an alcove, or had been an alcove bed – a *lit en niche*. This was recreated by building a large walk-in cupboard on the right. The woodwork was done in a pale green, which toned well with the striped wallpaper in two tones of sandy yellow. Laura used an early nineteenth-century English chintz for the bed alcove curtains, the green being picked up by the tasselled trim. She was particularly fond of Biedermeier furniture and used a number of pieces

Bernard's desk in his
study. The framed picture
of two soldiers is an early
placemat.

Bernard's study. The
bookcases to the left were
designed to take his files.
The walls were in grey
moiré-effect paper and a
matching fabric was used
for the curtains, with their
Flemish headings or goblet
pleats.

here, the pale tone of the wood working well with the pale
background paper.

Bernard's bedroom was a mirror image of Laura's and
decorated in a similar style. Instead of the floral chintz a
vine-leaf print was used, trimmed with blue bullion; a lighter
smoke blue was used on the skirtings and other woodwork.
In the principal guest bedroom the Ashleys copied the design
of the bed canopy from the state bed at Inverary Castle in
Argyllshire. The bed was hung with a striped floral chintz
trimmed with moss-green bullion, the pinks and reds of the
chintz being picked up by the striped sofa at the foot of the
bed. The room is unmistakably English, but with the odd
dash of French flavour, notably from the large armoire found
in the attic.

These houses all seemed to have larger rooms and
grander spaces than most of their customers' homes, but
the company had begun to do up houses especially for
catalogue photo shoots. The London house at 23 Campden
Street was one example, as was Upton Lodge near Tetbury
in Gloucestershire. This house was created in 1934 from
three estate cottages to form a comfortable residence for
the daughter of the great house, not far away. It had the
appearance of a cottage but this belied its size, for it had ten
bedrooms and six rooms on the ground floor. Laura, together
with the company stylist Sasha de Stroumillo, decorated
the house using that year's catalogue and the 'Decorator
Collection' to provide room sets for the 1983 and subsequent
catalogues. It also resulted in a small paperback book, *A
House in the Cotswolds*, written by Jane Clifford.

The heavy oak front door opened into a small hall
and corridor leading to the staircase and library beyond.
The stone-flagged floor and oak beams were key to the
decoration and for the hall and corridor they used a small
pattern wallpaper called 'Dog Rose'. Beyond the staircase
was the library, or bookroom, and here they used a larger
scale patterned wallpaper called 'Oak Tree', derived from a
sixteenth-century Italian design. They linked the two spaces

ABOVE LEFT: The hall at Upton Lodge, papered in 'Dog Rose', a small pattern used as a prelude to the library.

LEFT: 'Oak Tree', used in the library.

RIGHT: The library.

together by using 'Dog Rose' for the curtains with their castellated pelmet. This simple brown and cream decorative scheme was a good introduction to the house and allowed the other rooms to work effectively.

The drawing room opened off the hall and was done in blue. A blue and white striped paper was used with a plain light turquoise Wilton carpet, strewn with Persian rugs. The room was decorated in an early Victorian manner; Victorian, with a dash of Regency flavour. The room was dominated by a large low backed sofa, with a multi-coloured floral satin cotton used for the loose cover, the same fabric used for the cottage style curtains, with a soft valance and frilled edge backlined in the blue and white stripe to match the walls. A large circular table, which actually hid the television, was covered by a tablecloth, again in the same fabric drawn from the 'Decorator Collection'.

The dining room remained much as it was in the nineteenth century, the only change seems to have been the addition of a small stone fireplace in 1934. The Ashleys had the walls painted in a golden tan shade – their own paint 'Light Tan' – with curtains in a simple crimson and yellow stripe, edged by bullion fringe. A window seat and cushions were done in a small print, 'Wild Clematis', in plum and cream.

Opening off the dining room a circular staircase lead to the bedrooms. The main bedroom was over the library. It was furnished with old oak and walnut pieces, mostly dating from the late-seventeenth and early-eighteenth centuries. But all was not what it seemed. Using a piece of old panelling, the company workshop created a four-poster bed, with bedposts made from nothing more complex than three-by-three fencing posts and six-by-one pine planking stained up to the colour of old oak for the framing. The bed was hung with 'Periwinkle' (F6), a striped fabric with a trailing pattern in one stripe, with a small rosebud in the other stripe and lined in a pink and white pattern called 'Clover' (F43). The small rosebud was used as wallpaper ('Rosebud' F5) with the small periwinkle-like design (actually 'Rose Multi White' F7)

ABOVE: The dining room laid
for dinner. The walls were
painted in the company's
paint 'Light Tan'.

used as a border. A small adjacent room of rather an awkward shape was turned into a dressing room, furnished with a few Dutch marquetry pieces, and the room was papered with 'Scottish Thistle' (F4) in burgundy printed on cream. The sage bathroom was papered in one of the most popular patterns, 'Nutmeg' (S49), in cream and sage, with the colours being picked up by the curtains in a large floral design printed in green and cream.

At the north end of the house was the Lavender bedroom. They used a very Victorian looking wallpaper of stripes, drawn from the 'Decorator Collection', the pattern being repeated for the bedspread. A small floral design was used as a contrast in the curtains and bed valance and also for the corona and its associated curtains. Laura picked up Victorian details by adding a frilled edge to the curtains, itself bound by a lavender edging tape.

On the second floor, reached via the old circular stair, were yet more bedrooms of which the most striking was probably the Trellis room, so named after the 'Trellis' paper (P768) printed in moss green on cream. This was used in conjunction with a floral chintz in dense reds and greens, again drawn from the 'Decorator Collection', and used for the curtains and bedspread. All together it created a rather masculine room.

In the same year, Laura and Bernard acquired a house in the South of France near Var, as a summer residence, and in the spring of 1985 they bought the Villa Contenta at Lyford Cay in the Bahamas for the winter months. In late 1984 they rented a house in Palm Beach, Florida, which was decorated and used for the 1986 catalogue, with the hall, veranda and three rooms illustrated. The house was not by Addison Mizner, the great name in South Florida architecture, but was in his style.[26] These Spanish colonial houses required a quite different treatment from most of the houses they usually worked on. The light in Florida is brighter and stronger than in Britain, so the colours of the fabrics were brighter and stronger. The hall was quite plain, with a black and white

tiled floor, and the arched windows simply dressed with a grey and white striped cotton called 'Cirque' (F782). In the dining room the walls were painted a sapphire blue over which they placed white diamond trellis, a treatment that is still popular in Florida today. The curtains were a bold vertical stripe called 'Carousel', in a strong blue and white with simple frilled pelmets. Mizner's influence is more clearly visible in the drawing room, which was panelled with bleached Floridian pecky cypress. The floor of glazed terracotta Spanish tiles was faintly reminiscent of a villa in Tuscany. The sofa and chair were in a plain dobby weave, while the two slip chairs were upholstered in 'Fretwork', a blue and white cotton which was also used for the curtains. More pattern was introduced by cushions in 'Chinoiserie', a Chinese pattern chintz. In the bedroom another Chinoiserie inspired fabric – this time 'Crystal' (F784) – was used for all the curtains. Drawn from a design by Crace & Co. for the Prince Regent's Royal Pavilion at Brighton in 1803, it combines stripes of flowers on a diamond trellis background. The rich red colouring lived happily with the heavy Spanish colonial mahogany bed.

Laura was also involved in the decoration of another house: not a family residence but a museum house in Williamsburg, Virginia. The project had a dual function: it served as a showcase for some of the company's products and also demonstrated how Victorian patterns and objects could be blended and used in the modern world. Miss Dora's House was also an opportunity for Laura to give something back to the American people in thanks for their abundant kindness to her and her family. America had by then become a huge market for Laura Ashley products.

In April 1985 Laura spent a day going over the house. A huge quantity of family posessions remained and she carefully examined and labelled everything, allocating them positions within the house. Laura remarked: 'Most of us live together with one or more pieces of furniture from other times – old books, china, pictures – and this greatly influences our other choices.'[27] She appointed Arnold Copper, a Virginian-born designer, to oversee the project in her absence. All the wallpapers and fabrics used were from the Laura Ashley ranges, and what is remarkable about the house is the sense of period that was created, and that there is also something specifically American about the interiors, even though some of the patterns used, such as the Owen Jones wallpaper in the parlour, are decidedly English.

The house opened to the public in May 1986. It remained so for about twenty years, before the property was sold. Standing on Duke of Gloucester Street, adjacent to the Governor's Palace, the Victorian house struck a discordant note as eighteenth-century Colonial Williamsburg was recreated all around it. The owners, the Armistead family, had refused many overtures from the Rockefellers' agents, and the Colonial Williamsburg Foundation were only finally able to acquire the property after the millennium. It has now been moved half a mile and the eighteenth-century coffee house, upon whose foundations the house had stood, rebuilt in its stead.[28] Laura's work is, alas, no more, but at least the house was photographed.

Laura and Bernard learnt the art of interior decoration as they went along. As their knowledge grew, their tastes gradually changed, but they remained firmly rooted in the Victorian era: 'I didn't set out to be Victorian but it was a time when people lived straightforward, basic lives, when everything was clear cut and respectable .... Respectability matters a lot to me.'[29] Quite often Victorian pattern, design and decoration gets a bad name, usually undeservedly so, for any careful study of the period reveals an abundance of riches, which we might use. The trick is, as with all decoration, to edit and select. Laura's houses show that she was a judicious editor.

ABOVE: The lavender bedroom in Williamsburg papered in 'Meadowsweet' (see page 106).

RIGHT: The trellis bedroom on the top floor. The floral chintz was drawn from the 'Decorator Collection'.

ABOVE: The Ashley children
on the terrace at Rhydoldog.
From the left, Nick, Jane,
Emma and David.

TRIUMPH AND TRAGEDY

In April 1979 the company celebrated its silver jubilee. The Ashleys returned home to Wales for the first time in a year. To mark the celebrations they gave a huge silver anniversary ball with 700 guests at the Deeside Leisure Centre in Queensferry, Flintshire, not far from Chester. Entertainment was provided by the Royal Artillery Band, and Sir Harry Secombe brought the house down with that familiar Welsh favourite, *We'll keep a Welcome in the Hillside.* The entertainments concluded at 2 a.m. with everyone linking hands and singing *Auld Lang Syne.* After twenty-five years the company had a turnover of more than £25 million, and after just eleven years in the retail business it had over seventy shops.

In the same year they began to open shops in Sainsbury's Homebase do-it-yourself chain. This was a new departure. Chance had played a part in this development – it was all down to an event that had occurred years before. A lady had walked into the Sloane Street shop in London looking for fabric. She found something she liked, a sand coloured fabric with a small black motif, and rather surprised the assistant by asking for 300 yards. This was a Tuesday, the fabric arrived on Friday morning and was collected on Saturday. Every other shop the customer had tried had put her off with long delivery dates. Years later Laura Ashley were invited to open shops within Homebase. It turned out that the customer's husband was a director of Sainsbury's.[1]

The business grew at an astonishing rate, and at home the children were also growing up fast. It was probably inevitable that the Ashley children would all become involved in the business, and it is interesting to note that they all possess an eye for design inherited from their parents. When Jane reached eighteen her father bought her a Pentax camera and appointed her company photographer. She was told to get on with it, which was typical of Bernard's style of management. Jane proved herself a very skilful and innovative photographer, and she developed a unique style, producing atmospheric publicity shots. It was Jane's publicity photographs that helped to shape the Laura Ashley public image, and even today her photographs are visually striking. Looking back on those years today, Jane is 'very proud of all we achieved together as a family business, and of the part I played in that, and not just in creating the visual imagery with my photographs. It was a traditional concept: a family run business that worked particularly well in the factory in mid-Wales; the legacy of hard work and fun (an agenda set by my parents) which the business was built upon, remains to this day.'[2]

The eldest son, David, seemed to have inherited his father's love of machines. He went off to study engineering, securing an apprenticeship at a firm in Newtown, much to his father's disgust as he thought his son could learn all that was necessary at the factory in Carno. In 1975 David was sent to help run the American arm of the company. They had opened their first shop in Jackson Square in San Francisco in 1974. It had not been an overwhelming success. The United States has more often than not been a graveyard for British retailers, and Laura Ashley could quite easily have been yet another case in point. Jackson Square was a poor location. Situated in the financial district, it was a large basement which had – almost unbelievably – no shop front. How customers were expected to find the shop, let alone be enticed in, was a mystery. After a first flush of enthusiasm, it soon became obvious that the site was problematic and difficult for customers to find. The losses mounted until eventually it was costing $5,000 a month to stay open.[3] Bernard was all for closing and cutting their losses, but they were tied into the lease.

Eventually Jean and Peter Revers went out to run the US side. Jean had been taken on to manage the Shrewsbury shop, after an initial false start. Bernard had turned up unexpectedly to find the new shop a mess and the staff sitting around smoking. He sacked the lot of them, but was eventually persuaded to give the shop a second chance, and appointed Jean as manageress. He was impressed by her determination and by the fact that her husband Peter – who was not employed by the company at the time – helped her turn the shop around. Bernard rescued Peter from the tedium of selling Mars bars in Yorkshire and Lancashire, offering him a job helping to market furnishing fabrics, which he was just relaunching.

Peter and David Ashley decided to make the brand more exclusive for the US market. This was partly dictated by American import duties on garments. The fancy detailing attracted a 35 per cent duty, and then there were the freight charges, so it made sense to aim the products at a more upmarket clientele. In 1977 they opened another shop, this time on Madison Avenue in New York, which became the company's US flagship store. One of David's first jobs was opening a store in Boston and he had developed a formula for the store design, and in fact became a very talented shop designer. He also had a natural grasp of the American market, which is often viewed as one gigantic whole, but which is in fact several different markets, often divided by climate.

The youngest son, Nick, was to become heavily involved with the company and would work closely with Laura on a day-to-day basis. He left school without any qualifications – a chip off the old block one might say – and then went to Paris, supposedly attending art college, but spending more time

hanging out 'with a load of bikers'. Returning to England he spent some time at St Martins School of Art studying whatever he wanted as he was never officially a student but merely turned up and got in via the back door. In the afternoons he worked as a 'trotter' for the tailor Tommy Nutter. After that he worked for a while in the art department of *Vogue*, finally joining the business in 1980. 'My dad said to me, "You can either start from the top or the bottom", which I thought was a bit of a stupid question. I was taken on as design director.'[4] His first job was to design a catalogue and, having come hot foot from *Vogue*, suggested they make it like a magazine, which is what happened.

Nick was young and brimming with ideas. One of the best-selling fabrics in 1983 was 'Emma', a bold splash print he commissioned and named after his younger sister to mark her eighteenth birthday. In 1982, looking for a new project after the success of the catalogue, he approached the Charleston Trust about reproducing some fabrics designed in the 1930s by the artists Duncan Grant and Vanessa Bell.

It was a logical development, continuing the 1920s theme of the fashion collection launched in the winter of 1982. It also continued the 'Brideshead look', then all the rage, but in design terms it broke away from the traditional Laura Ashley image, and offered customers something new and strikingly different. Eventually a deal was struck and the company created faithful reproductions of a number of fabrics for the house. This was easier said than done. Nick eventually found a source in Germany for some slub rayon, the material originally used in the 1930s. The main concern however was getting the colours exactly right. Unpicking some hems they were able to obtain tiny samples of the original colours, but in the event it was decided to compromise and reproduce the fabrics in shades halfway between the washed out, badly faded colours, and the original bright garish shades. The patterns that eventually went into commercial production, marketed as the 'Bloomsbury Collection', were slightly re-scaled and re-coloured and then printed on linen union rather than narrow-width rayon. To complement the collection Nick

OPPOSITE: A Bloomsbury room set, a reconstruction of a music room originally designed by Vanessa Bell and Duncan Grant which was exhibited at Lefevre Gallery in London in 1933. The curtains are 'Charleston Grapes' in grey, with the box pelmet in 'Charleston Border'.

ABOVE: Another room set, created in a house in west London for the 1987 catalogue. The wallpaper is 'Waves' and 'Bloomsbury' is used for the curtains, with a pelmet in 'Charleston Border' only this time with pleats.

LEFT: A Welsh cottage kitchen before it was restored for a publicity shoot for Laura Ashley.

ABOVE: The cottage kitchen as decorated for the shoot. The wallpaper is 'Cherries' and was featured in the 1986 catalogue.

also commissioned designs for a fruit bowl, vase and fruit plate from Quentin Dell, Vanessa's son.[5]

Emma, like her siblings, inherited Laura's eye for design, but also her father's flair as an entrepreneur, cadging new dresses, which she sold on at school. She would take the firm's party frocks and cut them down to give them a more 'fashionable' hemline. Emma did point out that none of her school friends wore Laura Ashley clothes – they were perceived as far too fuddy-duddy, old fashioned, all frills and lace; really the sort of thing granny wore. Laura asked Emma to make a few suggestions. So from the age of fourteen Emma would send the design team sketches, all coloured and with suitable fabric suggestions. The result of her initial sketches and ideas was known as 'Emma's collection', designed for girls aged twelve to fourteen, and included dresses, skirts and shirts, all useful school wear, and dungarees and party frocks. They were all in plain and printed cotton in bright attractive colours. Dungarees, which may seem a very radical departure, had first appeared, probably at Emma's suggestion, in 1979/80.

With Nick involved in the business Laura was able to withdraw slightly from the day-to-day design work. She continued to research prints and maintained an extensive design library at the chateau. In Paris Laura made use of the Musée des Beaux Arts and enjoyed rummaging amongst the antique shops on the Left Bank. She also loved visiting the Musées des Tissus et des Arts Décoratifs in Lyon. Living in Brussels and at the chateau, Laura's tastes gradually changed. She still had an almost uncanny knack of being able to select commercially viable patterns, but her eye was drawn to grander more imposing fabrics. She recognized that many of these grander patterns would be unsuitable for her core customers, and this was where the idea of the 'Decorator Collection' (as mentioned in chapter four) came in. Laura recognized that the interior decorators who bought from the shops were always looking for something new and distinctive. You only needed one of them to use a new pattern

Style BL254 Saxe Blue.

Style BL254 Clover

Style BL254

This popular blouse in 100% cotton lawn, with tucking detail on the front bodice and neat frills on the collar and sleeves, is offered in pure white and two colours to co-ordinate with the rest of the Collection.
Sizes: 10, 12, 14, 16.
Colour: White.
Price: £13·55 plus p&p.
Colours: Clover or Saxe Blue.
Prices: £13·95 plus p&p.

Style DG3

These cool comfortable dungarees in 100% cotton, with adjustable straps, optional belt, and two handy seam pockets, are offered in toning stripes in either soft or bright combinations. Fun dressing for all age groups and a fashionable maternity outfit.
Sizes: S, M, L.
Colours: Soft or Bright.
Prices: £17·95 plus p&p.

Style DG3 Soft

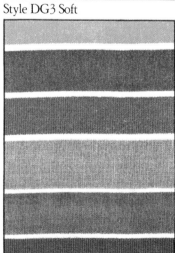

Style DG3 Bright

Styles BL254 & DG3

173

and for it to be featured in a glossy magazine and it would soon be a fashionable design, particularly when produced at the advantageous Laura Ashley price. This would make it affordable for Laura's natural customers. It was a case of trying to lead her customers and develop their tastes but, as mentioned previously, many of her customers were slow to change their preferences.

As Laura Ashley became well known and gained what in marketing circles they call name recognition, other people wanted to be associated with the company. They had received a number of approaches from cosmetics manufactures to market perfume and other products bearing the Laura Ashley name. Naturally Bernard decided to do it himself. He approached the Swiss perfumers Firmenich to help and Charles Firmenich, with his legendary nose, came to see Laura. They studied Laura and came up with two different perfumes, both of which she liked, so they introduced them as Number 1 and Number 2. The perfumes were produced in France and nicely packaged in a floral box designed by Nick. They were very successful and extremely profitable. This success prompted them to produce other ranges like talcum powder, bath salts, and soap. These were also successful, which was

just as well. The employee responsible for ordering the soap inadvertently ordered 50,000 bars rather than the 5,000 she had been instructed to buy. Honesty is always the best policy, so when the mistake was discovered she reported it straight to Bernard and offered her resignation. It was declined. All Bernard wanted to know was the projected sales rate and how long would it take to sell the extra 45,000 bars.

The 1970s had brought the Ashleys huge success and an enviable lifestyle, but times were changing. An exhausted Labour government was swept from office in May 1979, ushering in an energetic and reforming Conservative administration under Britain's first woman Prime Minister, Margaret Thatcher. One of the things she set out to do was to reform the public sector, and in November 1984 there began a series of privatizations of state industries with the sale of shares in British Telecom. Other privatizations were to follow and, together with many conventional share flotations, these increased the public's interest in the financial markets, which the government eventually liberalised and reformed with what was known as 'big bang'.[6] It was against such a background that the Ashleys were advised to float the business on the London Stock Exchange. Bernard was all for the idea. They were advised that it was not a good idea for the entire family fortune to be concentrated in one thing, and most certainly not a textile and fashion business. Floating the business would enable the family to diversify some of their wealth. Laura was implacably opposed to the whole idea. To her it was, perhaps not a betrayal of the philosophy of the company, but contrary to what it stood for and certainly a diminution of those ideals and values.

The Ashleys had already left Britain to live abroad in 1977, basically because of the tax system. Their absence and restricted ability to visit the United Kingdom – they could only visit for ninety days a year – had meant a change in the structure of the company. It had grown far too large to be run in the friendly ad-hoc manner that had previously very much been the norm. Organising the company for flotation took

time and required a radically different corporate structure. Bernard was never very keen on bank managers and Laura was never very keen on accountants, whom she regarded with the utmost suspicion. Preparing the business for floatation required an army of accountants. One employee drily observed that 'the accountants arrived like undertakers', and given what eventually happened to the company the remark showed a remarkable degree of perception.[7] Bernard was to recall: 'I blame myself: Laura was absolutely right. We should never have floated the company.'[8] The public flotation, which Laura had so adamantly opposed, went ahead on 5 December 1985, and was in the short term a great success. In the 1990s however, the company experienced serious financial difficulties. In 1998 Malaysian investors came to the rescue and acquired a controlling interest in the company. The judgement of hindsight, and of history for that matter, is often harsh but it is seldom as harsh as we are likely to be about our own failings or errors.

Though Laura worked incredibly hard, she never felt successful, but success in fashion is always fleeting and transient. You're only as good as your last collection. What interested both Laura and Bernard was getting the concept right and making it work: it wasn't about making money as such. Laura was never very materialistic, and in fact she found her wealth more of an embarrassment. Sir Terence Conran, who was an old friend, found himself travelling to New York on the same flight as Laura one day. She offered him a lift, as there would be a car waiting for her at the airport, but was very embarrassed when the car in question turned out to be a stretch limousine.[9] This was entirely characteristic of Laura: she wasn't interested in jewellery, nor in fine clothes, even though she could well afford both. She would buy clothes from Jean Muir, Saint Laurent and Jaeger, often surreptitiously snipping the label out so Bernard wouldn't know. Her style was surprisingly understated, preferring as she did plain colours and quite simple designs, maintaining the same basic wardrobe at all their houses.[10] It was a sort

of uniform. She observed: 'I'm too involved with them [the company's clothes] and prefer to stand back from my own designs.'[11] She did love the chateau and its gardens, more for its inherent beauty than the status or the grandeur of owning a French chateau. In that part of France every other house in the neighbourhood was called a chateau. Even though she loved Remaisnil she remarked to her daughter one day, not long before she died, 'I could walk away from all this today with just a rucksack on my back.'[12]

Laura did not want any fuss to mark her sixtieth birthday on 7 September 1985. She and Bernard came over to England to a board meeting and to visit Jane, their elder daughter who had just given birth to another grandchild. Laura spent the afternoon pottering around Moreton-in-the-Marsh with her daughter. She went to bed early at about 10 p.m., and around 4.30 a.m. got up. Not wishing to disturb the rest of the house, she walked out of the guestroom without turning on the landing light and, mistaking the stairwell for the bathroom, she fell down the stairs. Bernard, hearing a loud crash, got up to find Laura lying at the bottom of the stairs: 'She was already dead, but we didn't realize this at the time.'[13] She was rushed to Walsgrave Hospital in Coventry where she died nine days later on Tuesday, 17 September 1985.[14] It was a tragic, pointless and senseless accident. The family were devastated and as Jane recalled: 'Our lives changed forever with the death of our Mother; maybe that's always the case with untimely deaths. She was such a wonderful and inspiring person and it has been very hard to come to terms with. She is still greatly missed.'[15]

Her funeral was held a few days later on the Friday at the church of St John the Baptist in Carno, a few yards from the factory. The vicar, fearing his stamina might not be equal to the required peddling, wisely imported an electric organ for the day to replace the push pedal harmonium that was normally used. The day was dull and overcast, and some of those who were present recall the silence and quiet of the day. Barely any traffic seemed to pass, even though it was a busy road, and at one point a freight train seemed to glide silently by. The press reported that a congregation of nearly 2,000 people gathered for the service, but as there were people standing on the hills the actual congregation was probably double that. The bier was adorned with wild flowers, gathered from the surrounding countryside and so familiar from the very fabrics with which Laura's name will be forever associated. In his address, Lord Hooson (the former member of Parliament for Montgomery and a close family friend) remarked that Laura was 'the most private of all the public people I have ever met', but to those who knew her she was 'charming and lovely'.[16] The Anglican service was partly conducted in Welsh, with some familiar hymns, and the Dowlais Male Voice Choir sang a Welsh hymn at the graveside. Laura was laid to rest amid the Welsh countryside, which had always been her greatest love and her greatest inspiration.

A few years later the family returned once more to St John's for a service of thanksgiving to mark the restoration of the spire. The original spire had been removed twelve years before because it was structurally unsafe; the restoration was financed by a donation from the Ashley children in memory of their mother. Nick explained, 'My Mother would not be happy with a church without a spire.' A computerized clock was installed, and the seventeenth-century bells were re-hung so they once more rang out across the valley just as Laura had remembered. It was a generous gift and complemented a substantial donation made the previous year by Sir Bernard towards the Carno Community Centre.

When Laura Ashley died in September 1985 the business that bore her name had a turnover well in excess of £100 million, more than 200 shops dotted around the world and employed over 4,000 people. For a business founded in 1953, a mere thirty-two years before, such a phenomenal rate of growth and expansion – which continued after Laura's death – was quite remarkable. And yet what is even more remarkable is that it all began on a kitchen table in Pimlico.

The story of Laura Ashley the company is inextricably linked to the lives, characters and personalities of Laura and Bernard Ashley, for this was very much a partnership and they always worked together as a team. Each brought complementary strengths and talents, and Laura Ashley the brand would never have existed without both of them. It was Bernard who brought the drive and the business acumen, and perhaps also some appreciation of colour and design, but it was Laura who had the taste, the eye and that almost magical ability to spot a trend or a fashion before it had become either. With Laura gone the heart went out if it for Bernard, which is perhaps understandable considering their whole lives were so closely linked and intertwined with the business.

Bernard, who was knighted in 1987, remained company chairman until 1993 (the company's fortieth anniversary) when he stepped down, remaining a director until 1998. He went on to develop a chain of luxury hotels – Ashley Inns – and finally returned to where he had started, founding a digital textile printing company, Elanbach Ltd., in 2001. He was fascinated by the possibilities of this new technology and it absorbed his interest until his death in February 2009.[17]

Shakespeare wrote in *Julius Caesar* that 'The evil that men do lives after them, the good is oft interred with their bones'. In the case of Laura and Bernard Ashley this is not true, for it is the good that lives on. It lives on in the fabrics and the fashions they created together. But perhaps more importantly the good lives on in the huge difference Laura and Bernard were able to make to so many people's lives. Laura and Bernard Ashley are remembered with deep affection in mid-Wales, and with a deep sense of pride and of gratitude. And surely there can be no finer memorial than that.

NOTES

CHAPTER ONE

1 Laura Ashley, interview with Sir Cliff Michelmore, BBC *Home on Sunday*, broadcast 1 July 1984.

2 Laura Ashley, interview with Jane Geniesse, *The New York Times*, 22 June 1978.

3 Laura's great grandmother had emigrated to the United States with her first husband. He died soon after they arrived in Boston, so she returned to Wales and married Lewis Benyon. Laura's parents were second cousins.

4 Laura Ashley, Sir Bernard Ashley, private papers.

5 Ibid.

6 Laura Ashley, interview with Sir Cliff Michelmore, BBC *Home on Sunday*, broadcast 1 July 1984.

7 Ibid.
In later life Laura could understand Welsh, although she could not speak it very well. Sir Bernard Ashley, interview with author, 7–8 December 2007.

8 Laura Ashley, interview with Sir Cliff Michelmore, BBC *Home on Sunday*, broadcast 1 July 1984.

9 The Twyniau Gwynion is the highest point in the Brecons.

10 Laura Ashley, interview with Sir Cliff Michelmore, BBC *Home on Sunday*, broadcast 1 July 1984.

11 Laura Ashley, Sir Bernard Ashley, private papers.

12 Laura Ashley, interview with Sir Cliff Michelmore, BBC *Home on Sunday*, broadcast 1 July 1984.

13 Admiral Ramsay had organized the Dunkirk evacuation and was responsible for the organization of the naval side of the Normandy landings. He was killed in an air crash in 1945.

14 Sir Bernard Ashley, interview with author, 7–8 December 2007.

15 Laura Ashley, interview with Sir Cliff Michelmore, BBC *Home on Sunday*, broadcast 1 July 1984.

16 Anne Sebba, *Laura Ashley: A Life by design* (Weidenfeld & Nicolson, London 1990), page 17.

17 Sir Bernard Ashley, interview with author, 7–8 December 2007.

18 Ibid.

19 *Observer*, 22 September 1985, page 50.

20 Bernard's father's family were originally Somerset farmers. There followed two generations of carpenters in Bristol. Geoff and Cornelia Ashley, interview with author, 8 December 2007.

21 Walter Seth Woodward was born at Southwell in Nottinghamshire in 1874. He married in 1900 and died, aged seventy-four, in December 1948. Bernard's grandmother married again in 1949 a John William 'Bill' Weed who was a retired Thames barge master.

22 The oil heater was used to heat the crude oil to make it sufficiently viscous so it could be jetted into the furnace. By the time Bernard came of age all the patents had expired and the company was a very small concern.

23 Sir Bernard Ashley, interview with author, 7–8 December 2007.

24 Ibid.
Oscar Wilde, *The Importance of Being Ernest*.

25 Sir Bernard Ashley, interview with author, 7–8 December 2007.

26 Tim Heald, 'Simple Patterns for Material Success', *Sunday Telegraph Magazine*, 27 January 1980, page 63.

27 Sir Bernard Ashley, interview with author, 7–8 December 2007.

28 A letter framed at Llangoed Hall from the Woman's Institute states that Laura started work with them in March 1949 and left in September 1952.

CHAPTER TWO

1 Sir Bernard Ashley, private papers.

2 Anne Sebba, *Laura Ashley: A Life by design* (Weidenfeld & Nicolson, London 1990), page 32.

3 Sir Bernard Ashley, interview with author, 7–8 December 2007.

4 Laura Ashley, interview with Sir Cliff Michelmore, BBC *Home on Sunday*, broadcast 1 July 1984.

5 Floral prints are often referred to as chintz. A chintz is a glazed fabric originally imported from India. The word chintz is derived from the Hindi 'chitra', meaning many-coloured or speckled. These fabrics were imported into Europe in the sixteenth century and were certainly known at the court of Queen Elizabeth I. By 1680 more than a million pieces of chintz were being imported into England per year, with similar quantities imported into France and Holland. The French banned their import in 1686, and England followed suit in 1720, but repealed the ban in 1774.

6 Screen rollers came in a variety of sizes – 25¼, 36, 42 inches and so on. Any design had to be a repeat of such a circumference. The pattern was picked out using an emulsion and the screen was baked to harden it. The process is now often done using lasers. Each screen probably cost upwards of £300 to create. Simon Maynard, Elanbach Fabrics, interview with author, 10 July 2008.

7 This customer had a small boutique in Knightsbridge. Sasha Schwardts, interview with author, 21 July 2008.

8 Sir Bernard Ashley, interview with author, 7–8 December 2007.

9 Sir Bernard Ashley, private papers.

10 Ibid.

11 Sir Bernard Ashley, interview with author, 7–8 December 2007.

12 Sir Bernard Ashley, private papers.

13 'Staff Remember the Old Days', *Laura Ashley News*, Issue 13, page 15.

14 Many of these early designs were Bernard's, but a few such as 'Circuit' and 'Plaza' were designed by John Sayers, an architect friend of Bernard's.

15 Elizabeth Dickson, 'Shopping Bureau', *Evening Standard*, 4 May 1960, page 8.

16 Sir Bernard Ashley, *The Rise and Rise of Laura Ashley*, ATV television, 1976.

17 Elizabeth Dickson, 'Shopping Bureau', *Evening Standard*, 4 May 1960, page 8.

18 Howard Bennett, telephone interview with author, 28 October 2008.

CHAPTER THREE

1 Ernestine Carter, 'In my Fashion: January', *Sunday Times*, 5 January 1969. They were described as 'an easy shift in navy and green awning striped cotton with three kangaroo pockets. Also in eight other colour combinations. 52*s*. 6*d*. at Dickens & Jones and Laura Ashley, 23 Pelham Street, SW7'.

2 Cristobal Balenciaga (1895–1972) experimented with the sack dress in the 1950s. He produced one in black wool for his 1959 Autumn collection, an example of which is now in the Victoria and Albert Museum dress collection (T.90-1973).

3 Jim Thorne, interview with author, 27 August 2008. It was Jim Thorne's mother who first became a friend of the Ashleys through the shop. She noticed Bernard's white Lotus and told her son, who at the time was obsessed with cars, that a man in the town had one. At the time the Thornes lived at Llancynfelyn about 10 miles away. The two families became friends, mixing in the same social circles – mostly English families who lived in the area.

4 Anne Sebba, *Laura Ashley: A Life by design* (Weidenfeld & Nicolson, London, 1990), page 55.

5 The popular perception of Welsh National dress – a red cloak and a tall black hat – is in fact a nineteenth century invention. The tall 'chimney' hat did not appear until the 1840s and is based on the top hat and a form of high hat worn in the country areas from the late 1780s until about 1820. Welsh countrywomen during the early nineteenth century often wore a striped flannel petticoat, under a flannel open-fronted bedgown, with an apron, shawl and kerchief or cap. The style of bedgown did vary from loose coat-like gowns, to gowns with a fitted bodice and long skirts, or the short gown, which was similar to a riding habit style.

6 Sir Bernard Ashley, *The Rise and Rise of Laura Ashley*, ATV television, 1976.

7 Sir Bernard Ashley, interview with author, 9 July 2008.

8 The first satellite factory was at Machynlleth, opened in a disused cinema in 1972. It had fifty-two machinists. Shrewsbury followed in 1973 and Oswestry in 1977. The first foreign factory opened in Wijk in the Netherlands in 1974, with a second at Helmond following two years later.

9 Although Paris is always regarded as the fashion capital of the world, the first haute couture house there is generally acknowledged to have been Worth's, whose founder, Charles Frederick Worth, was actually an Englishman, born in Lincolnshire in 1825. He was appointed court dressmaker to the Empress Eugenie in 1860. He died in 1895, but the business continued until 1953 when it was taken over by the House of Paquin.

10 Mary Quant was christened 'high priestess of sixties fashion' by Bernard Levin in his book *The Pendulum Years* published in 1970.

11 The Mini was launched in 1959 but was not actually christened 'Mini' until 1961. The car became an icon of the 1960s, particularly after it was used in the film *The Italian Job* in 1969. British Leyland also produced a car called the Maxi from 1969.

12 Barbara Hulanicki, telephone interview with author, 24 March 2008.

13 Ibid.

14 Raymond 'Ossie' Clark was born in Warrington in 1942. During the war his parents moved to Oswaldtwistle in Lancashire, hence his nickname 'Ossie'. He attended the Regional College of Art in Manchester (now Manchester Metropolitan University) where he met Celia Birtwell, whom he eventually married in 1969. Celia Birtwell was a fabric designer and their creative collaboration was one of fashion's most successful. Quorum was bought by the fashion house Radley, run by Albert Radley, in 1968, rescuing it from bankruptcy. Radley made Ossie's clothes available to a much wider clientele. Ossie and Celia divorced in the 1970s and his career began to decline. Although he worked again for Radley in 1984, his style was by then out of fashion. This gradual downward spiral came to a tragic end in August 1996, when Ossie Clark was murdered.

15 Brenda Polan, 'Materially Different', *Daily Telegraph*, 2 July 2007.

16 Laura Ashley, interview with Fyfe Robertson, BBC Wales, 1976.

17 Sir Bernard Ashley, interview with author, 7 December 2007.

18 The shop was in partnership with Philip Pollock, who was a partner of Terence Conran (his father designed the Marble Arch Odeon Cinema) and Angela Boyce (Angela Gore) who sold nightdresses while the Ashleys sold dresses.

19 *The Rise and Rise of Laura Ashley*, ATV television, 1976.

20 *The Times*, 24 June 1968, page 7.

21 *The Rise and Rise of Laura Ashley*, ATV television, 1976.

22 Sir Bernard Ashley, *The Rise and Rise of Laura Ashley*, ATV television, 1976.

23 Sir Bernard Ashley, interview with Fyfe Robertson, BBC Wales, 1976.

24 Sir Bernard Ashley, private papers.

25 'The success secrets of Laura Ashley', interview with Bonnie Estridge, *Woman*, July 1973, page 20.

26 Nick Ashley, interview with author, 16 October 2007.

27 Laura Ashley, interview with Fyfe Robertson, BBC Wales, 1976.

28 Laura Ashley, interview with Sir Cliff Michelmore, BBC *Home on Sunday*, broadcast 1 July 1984.

29 Sir Bernard Ashley, interview with Fyfe Robertson, BBC Wales, 1976.

30 Laura Ashley, interview with Fyfe Robertson, BBC Wales, 1976.

31 Sir Bernard Ashley, interview with author, 7–8 December 2007.

32 *The Forsyte Saga* was based on John Galsworthy's (1867–1933) novels: *The Man of Property* (1906); *Indian Summer of a Forsyte* (1918); *In Chancery* (1920); *Awakening* (1920) and *To Let* (1921). The series was broadcast on BBC2 from 7 January to 1 July 1967 and then repeated on BBC1 from 8 September 1968. It attracted an audience of more than eighteen million and was subsequently sold worldwide. It was the last major British drama series to be shot entirely in black and white.

33 The style is sometimes known as the 'Directoire', so named after the Directory that ruled France during the second half of the 1790s; 'Empire' refers to Napoleon's 1804–1814/15 empire (although he was also First Consul between 1800 and 1804). 'Regency' is used to describe the period of George IV's formal regency between 1811 and 1820, but can be applied to his reign until 1830.

34 In the company archive is a cutting from *Elle* magazine of a model wearing the dress. The cutting is from 1974, but is not exactly dated.

35 'Staff Remember the Old Days', *Laura Ashley News*, Issue 13, page 15.

36 *Evening Standard*, 20 November 1970, page 24.

37 Catherine Drinkwater, 'Golden Comeback for the Cambrian Mills', *Western Mail*, 13 September 1977.

38 Anne Sebba, *Laura Ashley: A Life by design* (Weidenfeld & Nicolson, London, 1990), page 153.

39 *The Fabric of Society* was written in three months and contained over three hundred illustrations. Remarkably it had a total print run of 20,000 copies. It was produced by Studio Press Print Group Ltd. of Birmingham, who printed the Laura Ashley catalogues, but had never done a book before. Sarah Levitt, letter to author, 7 September 2007.

CHAPTER FOUR

1 Nick Ashley, interview with author, 16 October 2007.

2 Sir Bernard Ashley, private papers. The remark was made by John James

3 Before they acquired a step and repeat machine several versions of the same print would have to be pasted together by hand and photographed to form a single screen, which required a high degree of accuracy. Inevitably mistakes were made, usually revealed in the spacing between each separate print. The step and repeat machine made one repeat that was then extrapolated over the whole screen.

4 The fabric was used for curtains and upholstery and also printed up as a wallpaper in a positive colourway (red on cream). It may have been named specially for the article, but was not in production in 1978. *House Beautiful*, August 1976, page 48.

5 Sir Bernard Ashley, interview with author, 7–8 December 2007.

6 Ibid.

7 'Staff Remember the Old Days', *Laura Ashley News*, issue 13, page 15.

8 Sir Bernard Ashley, private papers.

9 Owen Jones (1809–1874) was the son of a Welsh furrier and antiquarian. After an apprenticeship in an architect's office he travelled extensively in Italy, Greece, Turkey, Egypt and Spain. He made a special study of the Alhambra at Granada. He was one of the superintendents of works for the Great Exhibition held in 1851 and was responsible for the general decoration of the Crystal Place at Sydenham. He also set up the Museum of Manufacturers, the precursor to the Victoria and Albert Museum. Little of his work remains although some of his interiors done for Alfred Morrison at 16 Carlton House Terrace survive, as do some mosaics and capitals at Christ Church, Streatham Hill in London.

10 Ruth Weil and Jack Macurdy, 'A Rare Bit of Welsh', *House Beautiful*, August 1976, page 44.

11 Victoria Legge and Sasha Schwerdt, interview with author, 21 July 2008.

12 Christine Thompson, head seamstress at Chatsworth, interview with author, 15 July 2008.

13 Deborah, Dowager Duchess of Devonshire, letter to author, 2 June 2008.

14 Anne Sebba, *Laura Ashley: A Life by design* (Weidenfeld & Nicolson, London, 1990), page 188.

15 Christine Thompson, interview with author, 15 July 2008.

16 Laura Ashley, *The Rise and Rise of Laura Ashley*, ATV television, 1976.

17 Sir Bernard Ashley, 'The Nostalgia Business', interview with Fyfe Robertson, BBC Wales, August 1976.

18 Laura Ashley, *The Rise and Rise of Laura Ashley*, ATV television, 1976.

19 *Laura Ashley Home Furnishings Catalogue* 1981, (Laura Ashley Ltd, Carno, 1981), page 3.

20 Quite when Laura had lunch with John Fowler is unknown – neither of their diaries survive. The Ashleys knew Nancy Lancaster and had once dropped a bouquet of flowers at her home in Oxfordshire by helicopter with a card inscribed: 'To the finest decorator in the world'. David Ashley, interview with author, 9 July 2008; Barrie McIntyre, conversation with author.

21 Sir Bernard Ashley, interview with author, 7–8 December 2007.

22 Brian Uttridge, *Laura Ashley News*, Issue 12, page 6.

23 Laura Ashley, Introduction to *Laura Ashley Home Decoration*, 1983.

24 Robert Landgrebe, quoted in Anne Sebba, *Laura Ashley: A Life by design* (Weidenfeld & Nicolson, London, 1990), page 167.

25 The coding system used the car registration letter of that year. After producing 100 prints, the next print became the first print for the following year, so as a means of dating prints it is rather hit and miss. David Ashley, interview with author, 9 July 2008.

26 Elizabeth Dickson, 'Shopping Bureau', *Evening Standard*, 4 May 1960, page 8. Elizabeth Dickson joined the *Evening Standard* in July 1959 aged twenty-three. She moved on to *Vogue* where she was one of three fashion editors and ultimately became London editor for *Architectural Digest*.

27 Elizabeth Dickson, interview with author, 7 May 2008.

28 Ibid.

29 Sir Edwin Lutyens designed two houses with porticos: at the Ambassadors residence it is used on the garden façade, and at Gledstone Hall at West Marton in Yorkshire, built for Sir Amos Nelson in 1925, on the entrance façade.

30 Sir Bernard Ashley, interview with author, 7–8 December 2007.

CHAPTER FIVE

1 Jane Buchanan, telephone interview with author, 11 June 2008.

2 Anne Sebba, *Laura Ashley: A life by design* (Weidenfeld & Nicolson, London 1990), page 41.

3 David Ashley, interview with author, 9 July 2008.

4 Sir Bernard Ashley, interview with author, 7–8 December 2007.

5 Sir Bernard Ashley, Foreword, *Laura Ashley at Home: Six family homes and their transformation* (Weidenfeld & Nicolson, London, 1988), page 6–7.

6 Jim Thorne, interview with author, 27 August 2008.

7 Ibid.

8 Laura Ashley, Sir Bernard Ashley, private papers.

9 Jim Thorne, interview with author, 27 August 2008.

10 Laura Ashley, Sir Bernard Ashley, private papers.

11 Sir Bernard Ashley, interview with author, 7–8 December 2007.

12 Laura Ashley, Sir Bernard Ashley, private papers.

13 Ibid.

14 Ibid.

15 Ibid.

16 Martin Wood, *John Fowler: Prince of Decorators* (Frances Lincoln Ltd., London, 2008), page 115.

17 Laura Ashley, Sir Bernard Ashley, private papers.

18 Ibid.

19 *House Beautiful*, August 1976, page 47.

20 Laura Ashley, Sir Bernard Ashley, private papers.

21 Most complex patterns are built upon a pattern base. These bases take a number of different forms – squares, rectangles, diamond, ogee, are but a few.

22 *Laura Ashley at Home: Six family homes and their transformation* (Weidenfeld & Nicolson, London, 1988), page 40.

23 Laura Ashley, Sir Bernard Ashley, private papers.

24 *Laura Ashley at Home: Six family homes and their transformation* (Weidenfeld & Nicolson, London, 1988), page 68.

25 Jane Clifford, *Laura Ashley Decorates a London House* (Laura Ashley Ltd., Carno, 1985), page 6. The pattern book is in Manchester City Art Galleries.

26 Addison Cairns Mizner (1872–1933) was born in Benicia, California and was the son of a lawyer and diplomat. When he was forty-six he moved to Palm Beach in Florida and was commissioned to design the Everglades Club, still the most exclusive club in Southern Florida. He built many mansions in Palm Beach and his style was widely imitated and copied. The Ashley house was one such imitation.

27 *Laura Ashley at Home: Six family homes and their transformation* (Weidenfeld & Nicolson, London, 1988), page 127

28 Jim Brady, Press Officer Colonial Williamsburg Foundation, telephone interview with author, 14 February 2008.

29 Anne Sebba, *Laura Ashley: A life by design* (Weidenfeld & Nicolson, London, 1990), page 15

CHAPTER SIX

1 Sir Bernard Ashley, interview with author, 7–8 December 2007.

2 Jane Ashley, letter to author, 7 November 2008.

3 David Ashley, letter to author, 19 June 2008.

4 'Nick's Knack', *Sunday Times Magazine*, 23 October 1994, page 40.

5 Quentin Bell (1910–1996) was the son of Clive and Vanessa Bell. He was multi-talented, an artist, potter and sculptor who became a teacher, noted art historian and author. The novelist Virginia Woolf was his aunt.

6 The term 'big bang' was used in reference to the sudden deregulation of financial markets, which happened on 27 October 1986. The term was coined to describe measures including the abolition of the distinction between stockjobbers and stockbrokers on the London Stock Exchange. It abolished fixed commission charges and precipitated a complete alteration in the structure of the market. One of the biggest changes to the market was the change from open-outcry to electronic, screen-based trading.

7 Deborah James, telephone interview with author, 17 October 2007.

8 Sir Bernard Ashley, interview with author, 7–8 December 2007. The public flotation was a great triumph. The shares, offered at 135 pence each were thirty-four times oversubscribed. They opened at 186 pence and the following year touched 243 pence. Bernard retired from the company on its fortieth anniversary in 1993. Bernard was knighted in 1987 by Her Majesty the Queen for his services to industry.

9 Sir Terence Conran, interview with author, 4 August 2008.

10 Laura developed a sort of uniform of simple skirts and slightly more fancy blouses, usually with a raised collar, worn with fawn cardigans. This was partly because she travelled so much and with little or no luggage.

11 *The Sunday Times*, 16 June 1974.

12 Jane Ashley, interview with author, 3 November 2008.

13 Sir Bernard Ashley, interview with author, 7–8 December 2007.

14 The inquest was held on 9 October 1985. Mr David Sarginson, Her Majesty's Coroner for Coventry recorded a verdict of accidental death. He added that 'it could probably be assumed that Mrs Ashley had got out of bed in the middle of the night and fell because she mistook the stairwell for the bathroom next door'. *The Times*, 10 October 1985.

15 Jane Ashley, letter to author, 7 November 2008.

16 *Daily Telegraph*, 21 September 1985.

17 Sir Bernard Ashley married Regine Burnell, a Belgian photographer, in 1990.

BIBLIOGRAPHY

BOOKS

Ashley, Nick; Greene, Fayal; Haig, Catherine; Irvine, Susan; Jackson, Paula Rice, *Laura Ashley at Home* (Weidenfeld & Nicolson, London, 1988).

Berry, Susan, *Laura Ashley Decorating with Paper and Paint* (Ebury Press, London, 1995).

Berry, Susan, *Laura Ashley the Colour Book* (Ebury Press, London, 1995).

Clifford, Jane, *Laura Ashley Decorates a London House* (Laura Ashley Ltd., Carno, 1985).

Clifford, Jane, *A House in the Cotswolds* (Harmony Books, London, 1983).

Copestick, Joanna, *Laura Ashley Decorating Children's Rooms* (Ebury Press, London 1996).

Corbett-Winder, Kate, *Laura Ashley Living Rooms* (Weidenfeld & Nicolson, London, 1989).

Dickson, Elizabeth; Colvin, Margaret; *Laura Ashley Book of Home Decorating* (Octopus Books, London, 1982).

Dormer, Peter, *The Illustrated Dictionary of Twentieth Century Designers* (Quarto Publishing, London, 1991).

Egerton, Lucinda, *Laura Ashley Guide to Country Decorating* (Weidenfeld & Nicolson, London, 1994).

Evans, Deborah, *Laura Ashley Complete Guide to Home Decorating* (Weidenfeld & Nicolson, London, 1992).

Gale, Iain; Irvine, Susan; *Laura Ashley Style* (Weidenfeld & Nicolson, London, 1987).

Irvine, Susan, *Laura Ashley Bedrooms* (Harmony Books, London, 1988).

Jones, Owen, *The Grammar of Ornament* (Day and Sons, London, 1856).

McDowell, Colin, *McDowell's Directory of 20th Century Fashion* (Frederick Muller, London, 1984).

Mack, Lorrie; Egerton, Lucinda; Newdick, Jane; *Laura Ashley Guide to Country Decorating* (Weidenfeld & Nicolson, London, 1992).

Mack, Lorrie; Lodge, Diana; *Laura Ashley Decorating with Textiles and Trimmings* (Ebury Press, London, 1995).

Martin, Richard, *Contemporary Fashion* (St James Press, Detroit, 1995).

Sebba, Anne, *Laura Ashley: A Life by design* (Weidenfeld & Nicolson, London, 1990).

Strothers, Jane, *Laura Ashley: Decorating with Patterns and Textures* (Ebury Press, London, 1996).

Tozer, Jane; Levitt, Sarah; *Fabric of Society* (Laura Ashley Ltd., Carno, 1983).

Wilhide, Elizabeth, *Laura Ashley Windows* (Weidenfeld & Nicolson, London, 1988).

ARTICLES

Bowditch, Gillian, 'Where have all the flowers gone?', *Scotsman,* 22 July 2005.

Buck, Joan Juliet, 'Lady Henderson's Washington', *Vogue,* March 1980, page 158.

Carter, Ernestine, 'In my Fashion: January', *The Sunday Times,* 5 January 1969.

'Come Shopping', *Homes and Gardens,* June 1972.

Croft, Claudia, 'Laura, we love you', *The Sunday Times,* 6 January 2002.

Croft, Claudia, 'So then … so now', *The Sunday Times,* 28 April 2002.

Cubitt, Kirsten, 'Growing Organic Clothes', *The Times,* 22 August 1972.

Dickson, Elizabeth, 'Laura Ashley: Her life and gifts, by those who knew her', *Observer,* 22 September 1985.

Dickson, Elizabeth, 'Shopping Bureau', *Evening Standard,* 4 May 1960, page 8.

Drinkwater, Catherine, 'Golden Comeback for the Cambrian Mills', *Western Mail,* 13 September 1977.

Estridge, Bonnie, 'The Success Secrets of Laura Ashley', *Woman*, July 1973, page 20.

Fernard, Deirdre; Park, Margaret; 'After Laura', *The Sunday Times*, 4 February 1990.

Field, Leslie, 'Lady Henderson Moves House', *Panache*, November 1979, page 21.

Fitzgerald, Barbara, 'The Loose Look or Smock Alley', *Irish Independent*,14 May 1980.

Foltz, Kim, 'The Laura Ashley Touch', *Newsweek*, 17 September 1984, page 66.

Geniesse, Jane, 'Home Beat: Welsh, if you please', *The New York Times*, 22 June 1978.

Geniesse, Jane, 'At the British Embassy, a Stately renovation', *The New York Times*, 6 May 1982.

Glynn, Prudence, 'Prudence Glynn pays tribute to Laura Ashley', *The Sunday Times*, 22 September 1985, page 36.

Gould, Rachel, 'Laura Ashley Living', *Vogue*, 15 April 1980, page 122.

Groom, Avril, 'Laura's Look: Strictly No Frills', *Daily Telegraph*, 25 June 1979, page 13.

Hauptfuhrer, Fred, 'British Designer Laura Ashley turns a Victorian country look into a $60 million business', *Peoples Weekly*, 14 January 1980.

Heald, Tim, 'Simple Patterns for Material Success', *Sunday Telegraph Magazine*, 27 January 1980, page 63.

'How Laura Ashley took over a Chateau in Picardy', *House and Garden*, April 1980, page 138.

Keenan, Brigid, 'Out on a Limb', *The Sunday Times*, 8 July 1973, page 50.

Keenan, Brigid, 'Look! Fashion: Who is Laura Ashley?', *The Sunday Times*, 16 June 1974.

Kindel, Stephen, 'What do women really want?', *Financial World*, 8 December 1992, page 30.

Langdon, Dolly, 'Lady Mary Henderson saved a bundle for Britain by turning her Embassy into a Capital Showcase', *People Weekly*, 9 August 1982.

Laura Ashley News, July 1979 – August 1994.

Levine, Joshua, 'Wilted Flowers', *Forbes*, 10 April 1995.

Menkes, Suzy, 'Queen Cotton', *The Times*, 28 June 1983, page 9.

Menkes, Suzy, 'Earth mother of the alternative society', *The Times*, 18 September 1985, page 36.

'Nick's Knack', *The Sunday Times Magazine*, 23 October 1994, page 40.

Papworth, Veronica, *Sunday Express*, 2 July 1972.

Polan, Brenda, 'Materially Different', *Daily Telegraph*, 2 July 2007.

Price, Anne, 'The Magic of Dressmaker Clothes', *Country Life*, 22 June 1972.

Price, Anne, 'Be Valiant in Velvet', *Country Life*, 21 February 1974, page 398.

Raven, Susan, 'A life in the Day of Laura Ashley', *The Sunday Times Magazine*, 15 October 1978, page 126.

Salholz, Eloise, 'Here Comes Country Chic', *Newsweek*, 16 August 1982, page 42.

Scroggie, Jean, 'Shopping for an Indian Summer', *Daily Telegraph*, 16 August 1972.

Small, Michael, 'Cut from the same cloth as Mom and Dad', *People Weekly*, 24 September 1984.

'The Laura Ashley Look', *Brides*, Spring 1975.

'The Age to be: Laura Ashley's retreats', *Vogue Living*, August 1983.

Weil, Ruth; Macurdy, Jack; 'A rare bit of Welsh', *House Beautiful*, August 1976, page 44.

'Women's Feature', *The Times*, 24 June 1968 page 7.

OBITUARIES AND TRIBUTES

'Countryside funeral for Ashley', *The Times*, 21 September 1985, page 3.

'Laura Ashley', *The Times*, 18 September 1985.

'Laura Ashley: Restoring Romance to Fashion', *The Times*, 18 September 1985.

'Laura Ashley buried in Welsh village she loved', *Daily Telegraph*, 21 September 1985.

Laura Ashley Obituary, *Newsweek*, 30 September 1985, page 81.

Sir Bernard Ashley Obituary, *Daily Telegraph*, 16 February 2009.

'Sir Bernard Ashley', *The Times*, 17 February 2009.

Slesin, Suzanne, 'Laura Ashley, British Designer, is dead at 60', *The New York Times*, 18 September 1985.

INDEX

ACKNOWLEDGEMENTS

Life can so often be full of regrets, and it is one of my great regrets that I never knew nor ever met Laura Ashley. What a truly remarkable lady she was. I was fortunate enough to meet and in some small way get to know Sir Bernard Ashley. It proved to be a very rich and rewarding experience, for he was not only a dynamic and innovative businessman, but was also tremendously good company. He was what I often call a 'character', never dull or boring but stimulating company, interested in people and in the world around. He always had an opinion, which he expressed without fear or favour, and appreciated those who reciprocated in kind. He had a quick and ready wit, often finding humour at his own expense. I shall be forever in his debt for agreeing to help with this book (he was already an ill man) and for all his encouragement and

unstinting generosity. Alas Sir Bernard died on 14 February 2009, so he did not live to see the completed book, although he read every word of the text, merely correcting small errors of fact. We disagreed upon one minor point where he felt I had been too generous towards him. However, we discussed the matter and he graciously gave way, adding, with a wry smile, 'but I still think you're wrong'.

I would like to thank Lady Ashley for her continued help, and for her warm hospitality when I visited Sir Bernard. I am very grateful for all the help given by Laura and Bernard's children – Jane, David, Nick and Emma – who kindly spent considerable time talking to me about their parents and the Laura Ashley business. They searched for pictures, corrected facts and came up with all manner of leads and ideas. I am also deeply grateful to Geoffrey and Cornelia Ashley for their kind hospitality and assistance. It is Geoffrey Ashley who has helped to finish what his brother started and I am grateful for all his help.

This book could not have come to fruition without the help, support and encouragement of Laura Ashley Holdings Ltd and I would like to thank all the staff of the company. I would, however, particularly like to thank Lillian Tan, the Chief Executive Officer for granting me access to the Laura Ashley archive and for permission to use material found there. I am grateful to the archivists, Angela Jeffery and

Ann Parrotte for all they did in assisting with the research and also for helping to sort suitable illustrations. Their combined knowledge was invaluable. I would also like to thank the PR manager, Liz Owen for all her help and encouragement.

Thanks are also due to Tim Ardern for his kind hospitality on numerous visits to London, and to Helen and Robert Austin who very generously sponsored some of the travel pursuant to this book. I would like to thank Wayne English for his kind hospitality, for it was at his wonderful house on Patmos in Greece where much of this manuscript was assembled in an atmosphere of rustic simplicity and tranquillity.

I would very much like to thank the following for their help and assistance: Ari Ashley; Howard Bennett; Marianne Brace; Brewin Dolphin Securities Plc; June Buchanan; Charles & Terri Carroll, Chateau de Remaisnil; Mary Coates; Sir Terence Conran; Sheila Daniel, Cambrian Woollen Mill; Polly Devlin; the Dowager Duchess of Devonshire; the Duchess of Devonshire; Elizabeth Dickson; the Foreign & Commonwealth Office, London; Andy Garnett; Alan George; Ann Gore; Sir Nicholas Henderson; Barbara Hulanicki; Deborah James; Ros Jenkinson; Surapee Karnasuta; Dr Miles Lambert, Platt Hall; Dr John Lancaster; Victoria Legge; Sarah Levitt; the staff of Llangoed Hall, Llyswen, Wales; Barrie McIntyre; the staff of Manchester City Art Galleries; Simon Maynard and the staff of Elanbach Ltd; Caroline Noble;

Laura and Bernard in 1976

Meurig Price and the Dowlais Male Voice Choir; Sasha Schwardts; Anne Sebba; Juliet Still; Christine Thompson and the ladies of the Chatsworth sewing room; Jim Thorne; Malc Wood; the staff of Bradford City Libraries; Carlsbad Library and Oceanside Library, California, USA.

Finally I would like to thank the unseen and largely anonymous hands at Frances Lincoln Ltd. who make books a reality. They do a superb job, largely unthanked and unremarked upon, but let me make good this deficit. I am most grateful to the managing director, John Nicoll for commissioning this book; the publishing director Andrew Dunn; the designer Caroline Clark and my long-suffering editors Nicki Davis and Jo Christian. And finally, but by no means least, thanks are due to my literary agent, Catriona Wilson.

PHOTOGRAPHIC ACKNOWLEDGEMENTS

All the photographs in this book are the copyright of Laura Ashley Plc with the exception of those listed on this page. For permission to reproduce the images below, the Pulishers would like to thank the following:

Ari Ashley: 164, 118, 119, 120 (top), 128 (top), 129, 130 (bottom), 131, 132, 134, 135, 136, 137, 138, 139, 140

The Estate of Sir Bernard Ashley: 8, 11, 13 (left), 14, 15, 16, 17, 20 (top), 47, 86 (top), 110, 112, 113

David Ashley: 166

Emma Ashley: 28, 30, 116 (top)

Geoffrey and Cornelia Ashley: 35

Jane Ashley: 2, 38 (left), 49 (top), 52 (right), 59, 60, 63, 82, 179

CAMERA PRESS/ Charles de la Court: 79

CAMERA PRESS/ Peter Mitchell: 44

Charles & Terri Carroll, Chateau de Remaisnil: 141

The Trustees of the Chatsworth Settlement: 95 (top)

Elanbach Ltd: 22 (bottom)

Allan George: 6

John Lancaster: 20 (bottom), 21

MPTV/ LFI: 23

RBKC Library Service (photo John Bignell): 45

© Fritz von der Schulenberg – The Interior Archive (designer Laura Ashley): 146, 147, 148, 149, 154

Sasha Schwardts: 102, 103, 170, 171

V&A Images/ Victoria and Albert Museum: 39

Martin Wood: 9, 177 (bottom)

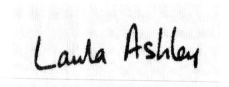

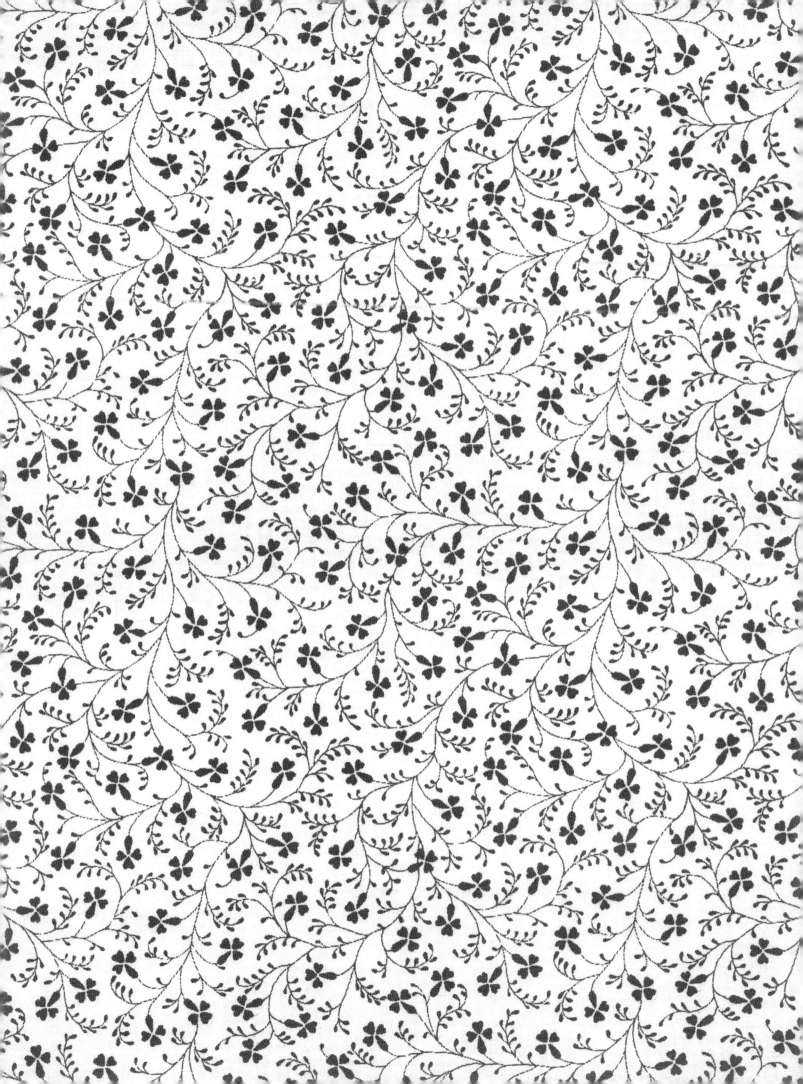